*How to Get the Most Out of
Clinical Pastoral Education*

How to Get the Most Out of Clinical Pastoral Education

A CPE Primer

Gordon J. Hilsman, D.Min
Foreword by Judith Ragsdale

Jessica Kingsley *Publishers*
London and Philadelphia

Epigraph on p.59 is reproduced with kind permission from the Journal of Pastoral Care and Counseling.

The ACPE standards are reproduced in Chapter 6 with kind permission from the ACPE.

First published in 2018
by Jessica Kingsley Publishers
73 Collier Street
London N1 9BE, UK
and
400 Market Street, Suite 400
Philadelphia, PA 19106, USA

www.jkp.com

Library of Congress Cataloging in Publication Data
A CIP catalog record for this book is available from the Library of Congress

British Library Cataloguing in Publication Data
A CIP catalogue record for this book is available from the British Library

ISBN 978 1 78592 793 5
eISBN 978 1 78450 782 4

Printed and bound in Great Britain

MIX
Paper from responsible sources
FSC
www.fsc.org
FSC® C013604

This book is dedicated to Bernard Pennington whose pointed validation of my perceptions, easy on-the-spot conceptualizing, and beckoning out my sleeping intuition were the building blocks of the second half of my life in a clinical pastoral education career.

Contents

Acknowledgements

B ooks are always the product of many people's efforts on various levels of contribution to the actual writing. From that point of view hundreds of people contributed to this book. I'll name a few whose contributions stand out in my creating of a primer for clinical pastoral education (CPE), the first I believe in the 90 plus years of the clinical ministry movement. The list of contributors starts with my own clinical supervisors and then briefly outlines my writing process. It took only six months to write this book, but consolidating my underlying convictions about CPE took over 40 years.

Orwoll (Oz) Anderson, the supervisor of my introductory unit of CPE in 1970, was a plain-spoken Midwesterner of Norwegian descent, who was both humanist and Lutheran to the core. It was his convictions about supervisory relationships and group leadership, unspoken but lived out, that sold me on CPE as a future career. I had been ordained for five years and was struggling with knowing that my theology was not enough when teaching religion to Catholic high school adolescents in any useful way. I also had become motivated by Teilhard de Chardin's evolutionary vision and saw it being played out boldly in that first CPE group. Thanks to you, Oz, for a transforming initiation into clinical education.

A corrections facility for youthful offenders in Wisconsin introduced me to supervisor Howie Johnson as I continued to try to understand adolescents—and in retrospect, my own adolescence— the following summer. His doggedly staying with the process of a very difficult peer student was admirable, memorable, and new for me. Could I do that with kids in a high school setting? Only partially I found. I headed for Chicago and Rush Presbyterian Medical Center a few years later to continue the pursuit of a kind of competence I couldn't quite even visualize at the time.

Bob Jais was a new supervisor there and into his own psychoanalysis during my third unit of CPE. From the beginning it felt like he liked me, believed in me, and used conveyed empathy masterfully, over and over with students, and incisive humor occasionally. There I realized that I was watching the supervisors' every move, scouring the culture for clues about how to do this myself someday. I'm grateful for Bob's natural giftedness and interest in me that kept the fires of supervisory aspirations glowing in me.

That same year I began supervisory education with Bernie Pennington who had trained several supervisors in the Chicago area already. He had a BA in literature, had completed his own psychoanalysis, and mastered the art of teaching concepts in the moment before I met him. His way of articulating supervisory theory in the midst of unfolding dynamics fed my mind just when such conceptual excellence was needed. We said goodbye to Bernie before his death at 47.

Joan Armstrong was Bernie's wife and a management level social worker in the department of psychiatry where I was assigned to work and learn as a supervisory student at Rush. She was my individual supervisor for several months in advanced and supervisory CPE, and she rather strikingly resembled my mother who had died when I was

20 years old. I'm grateful for the way she picked up on and amplified my strengths as a counselor in the addiction treatment program she directed, remedially filling some crucial holes in my parenting. Mom was a strong disciplined woman; Joan a sophisticated understanding one. That style of supervision turned out to be a major shaper of my own individual supervisory style.

My primary supervisor consultors for writing this primer—Sandy Walker, Melinda Holloway, and Paul Steike—used their sharp eyes, conceptual perspectives and quite different experiences of CPE on the text as it unfolded. Born in the 30s, 50s, and 70s, they represent eras of CPE that featured major growth of Association for Clinical Pastoral Education (ACPE) programming. My more regular consultors, Sandy Walker, Lisa Nordlander, and Wes McIntyre, let their critique flow as usual, regarding this writing. Thanks to all of them for calling my attention to major lacuna and unconscious slants in my own portrayed views which needed significant editorial attention.

Thanks to Carl Jensen whose Buddhist lens helped me find blind spots that were more visible to an outsider of Christian traditions. And thanks to John Patton for permission to quote him on theological reflection. This text would be quite different, and less useful, without their help.

Thanks to my wife Nancy and her patience with my writing mind that excludes her from my world for periods of time that are far too numerous and long. Finally, thanks to Judy Ragsdale for writing a quality Foreword, and to the publishing professionals at Jessica Kingsley Publishers who have always treated me like I deserve far more respect than I do.

Foreword

How to Get the Most Out of Clinical Pastoral Education: A CPE Primer is an outstanding orientation to this almost mystical process of education for spiritual care. This book explains the practices and the culture of CPE in evocative, clear language, making it both fun to read and eminently useful. Gordon begins this book outlining practical skills for spiritual caregiving and describes how the processes of CPE serve to perpetually develop the caregiver. He describes the culture of CPE, stressing its nature as process education, and offers helpful advice about what the CPE peer group is and how a CPE student might best use it for their learning.

Here are several sentences I particularly loved:

In describing the student's experience of facing a peer group, being expected to talk openly and extensively about their own single caregiving conversation, he says: "One way to conceptualize the optimal verbatim session attitude is to find a place on a continuum between the watertight stubborn and the sickeningly acquiescent."

He correctly believes that the verbatim group session is the key element in the CPE curriculum.

The author highlights the value of spiritual care education that uses real patient care experiences to educate, when he writes, "Becoming a quality caregiver of the human spirit is always jolting to a degree, as old ways of interacting and relating fall away, and new ones are created, almost with every new patient contact."

He emphasizes the group aspect of CPE in comments like, "helping one another become more thoroughly aware of and willing to share the flow of what is affecting each of them in the immediate situation may be the greatest gift of CPE peers to one another."

This is the only written work of which I'm aware that helps distinguish between entry level and an advanced level of CPE, and the process for making the transition between the two. A CPE Primer also describes an approach to writing final evaluations that will help me even at this point in my well-established practice, making this book useful for those seeking to engage in CPE as first-time students and for long-time certified educators alike. It goes on to speak about CPE as a path for spiritual development both for the student and for those the student serves.

A CPE Primer notes the limitations of the CPE method in such terms as "The ACPE's certifying arm has long strived to confirm a basic level of integration, skill, and identity before authorizing its educators to practice in its programs. That scrutiny is vigorous but not perfect." How true. Hilsman concludes with a chapter explaining what the various outcomes and objectives for Level I and Level II CPE—education for spiritual care providers—mean in practical terms. This chapter too will be helpful for CPE students and certified educators writing final evaluations. One such bit of guidance for Level II CPE Outcome 312.3 requiring "a range of pastoral skills" is: "Have they put together this quiver of competencies in an integrative way that allows them to be counted on to function consistently as a spiritual caregiver in a wide variety of situations?"

This book more than hints at the notion that care of the human spirit is a shared interdisciplinary responsibility and that this unique form of clinical education is for those practitioners of all professional helping disciplines who recognize the value of spiritual care for healing.

I met Gordon Hilsman when I was doing my PhD dissertation on ACPE Supervisory Wisdom, seeking to understand how experienced supervisors provided supervisory education. I received permission from those nominated as particularly adept at supervisory education to list their names at the end of the study. Gordon was one of what I have come to think of as "the wisdom supervisors." When I decided to put into practice the key learning from that study— that excellent supervision requires ongoing practise of vulnerably sharing one's work for consultation—I approached Gordon to be my consultant. We began a relationship of several years of me recording my supervision, sharing recordings with Gordon via Dropbox, and conferring with him about my supervision. First, we worked on my individual then group supervision of supervisory education students. Then, we moved on to consultation about my group supervision with fourth unit CPE residents. Gordon was consistently helpful and lived up to the guidelines he provides in this book. He did not offer empty validation or vague reflections, but carefully observed my practice and told me what he saw. Possibly the most useful advice he gave me was, "Stop telling the student what you want them to do; create an experience for them." I have found this useful advice in leadership situations as well.

Gordon loves CPE. He's good at it. Those who read this book stand to make better use of the CPE method if they attend to his guidance, taking what they need and leaving the rest.

With respect and thanksgiving for Gordon and this work.

Judith Ragsdale
November 21, 2017

Preface

U pon reading an early version of this book, a Buddhist chaplain educated in clinical pastoral education (CPE) remarked about the author, "He's giving away all the secrets!" Indeed, the way Association for Clinical Pastoral Education (ACPE) programs unfold, and the reasons why they do, may seem to have been intentionally kept secret. They have not. CPE is a process that unfolds differently every time it is conducted, making it extremely difficult to capture in its basic elements, just like romantic love and raising children. This book is an effort to do that in a way that is reasonably accurate and optimally helpful. There are three reasons why I am doing so now.

First is my belief that people considering application for an ACPE program will fare better, learn more, and better negotiate the transformative education needed for professional spiritual care functioning if they have a bare understanding of how it works, why it operates the way it does, and the benefits for investing time and effort in it. A most common story among ACPE supervisors, whom we now call certified educators, is how CPE transformed their lives by showing them themselves, confirming various perspicacious views of human beings and the kind of helping relationship they had already envisioned as optimal. This new place of authenticity, open disclosure, clearly conveyed empathy, and professional intimacy felt like the "real world," against the convoluted, often artificial-feeling milieu of religious organizations. If clearly describing the process of CPE, with its unique coalescence of highly personal encounter to radically improve self-awareness, can make it easier and more palatable for other would-be caregivers to enter it, then it is worth struggling to write such a book.

Second, ACPE programs are still evolving, and hopefully always will be. But there are essential elements of this unique cluster of educational methods that must not be lost to innovation and over-adaptation to perceived societal changes that may not be as positive as they look. CPE was one of the best human service inventions of the twentieth century, along with hospice, Alcoholics Anonymous, and social work. This book hopes to foster a preservation of that quality. What is old is not necessarily lesser in quality, as all who are influenced by any Sacred Scriptures know. Time will sort quality innovations from easier imitations. Meanwhile, this book represents the best of clinical spiritual care training, by the only association officially approved by the US Department of Education. Its basic elements need to be preserved and built upon, and this book contributes to that project.

Do not be put off by the names Freud and Jung if you hear them in CPE. It emerged when they were the rage in people-helping circles. They have not been so now for several decades because they missed the mark on several key aspects of humanity in their theorizing. But they ought not be dismissed easily just because we know more now than they did then. Newton knew nothing about quantum physics but created calculus as a top achievement of all time and it remains the foundation of engineering. The pivotal concept of the unconscious did the same for caregivers and it transformed society.

It is easy to forget that before the emergence of depth psychology, it was uniformly assumed that everything people do is conscious, intentional, and therefore inexcusable if errant from the norms of society. That one concept is key to self-exploration for improved self-awareness. It is not necessary to use psychoanalytic terms to conduct CPE. ACPE programs have substituted other terms for the process of radically improving self-awareness. Society would not allow people to work as physicians and nurses without a good measure of practice under supervision. Would-be spiritual caregivers with less than a year of CPE and a rigorous certification process remain much more likely to cause damage to people who are vulnerable in hospitalization.

Third, CPE needs to be extended to disciplines other than religious leaders. The lines between healthcare clinicians on the one hand, and spiritual caregivers on the other, are thankfully blurring in the area of spiritual care. Some of us certified educators believe that is a good thing. Spirituality is a universal aspect of all people, and like in other disciplines, some healthcare clinicians are more interested in and gifted for spiritual care than others. Those with the interest in providing crucial spiritual care to troubled people as part of the practice of their other disciplines, can benefit from this highly personal mode of learning, even though it has not yet doffed the term "pastoral." Granted, caring for religious struggles requires specialized preparation in faith group understanding and deep dedication to including transcendence as a central aspect of their care. But much of spiritual care that is necessary in the most trying times of life can be done by clinically trained and deeply committed spiritual practitioners of disciplines other than religious leadership. CPE is being offered to medical students at various places in the US as a fledgling effort in this direction.

My hope is that not only theology students and clergy persons shaken by life events will take the step to apply for these programs, but that those nurses, physicians, and social workers who harbor quiet fascination with the spiritual perspective on people, will do so as well. This book uses a pragmatic and humanist understanding of spirituality that can be used by serious caregivers of any discipline for the non-religious functions of spiritual caregiving. For every professional chaplain in the US there are now approximately 90 physicians, 260 nurses, and 30 licensed social workers. The growth of the palliative care movement in the past 20 years, and the hospice and addiction treatment movements as well, have shown how vital care of the human spirit is as a component of healing. A fair segment of those clinical professionals of other disciplines may find this book helpful in considering professional education for spiritual caregiving as a component of their practice.

The writing here represents ACPE programs as highly diverse and intentionally designed that way for richness of learning something useful about ethnic and national cultures, religions, age appropriateness, sexual orientations, and genders, and to parallel the populations of hospitals and other places of care in public institutions of a pluralistic society. CPE also discloses the need for some group members to inspect their own transcendence world view and consider augmenting it with what they learn from caring for patients while reflecting communally in the program. A new ACPE group member should know that they will be challenged as if they were learning to sail when they had been driving power boats all their life, or a kindergarten teacher now embarking on a medical career.

In reading this book you will notice that the terms "student", "group member", and "intern" are used interchangeably, according to which seems to best fit the context. "Group member" emphasizes that ACPE programs are always centered in small group dynamics. "Student" refers especially to the newness of this way of learning to most group members. The "intern" nuance highlights the parallel with medical education and the combination of learning and working needed in many fields to master their basics.

The reader also may notice that we mostly use the term "ACPE" instead of "CPE", referring to the community of educators that originated this method and which has worked for many decades to maintain its vigor and integrity. While there are several other professional associations that offer clinical pastoral education, with various differences in standards of operation and certification, the author is not knowledgeable enough about them to write about them in this primer.

Whether you're a pastor, a nurse, a physician, or an ancillary professional, you will be challenged in CPE, if you choose to hazard it, to let pained people affect you emotionally and respond in ways that guide, encourage, and inspire the human spirits of people to cope with and benefit from the natural tempests that eventually blow into every life. I hope this book will serve as a guide on that adventure.

Evolution is always impossible to recognize in the short term. It is a long and seemingly inefficient process. While we sort out which of the innovations in CPE circles are evolutionarily positive and which are merely the result of trying to make things easier for ourselves and look better to the world, we desperately need to preserve the methods of education that have led us to where we are today in the development of human care of humans. This book makes a contribution to that preservative project.

1

Engage the Educational Methods

On the first day of an ACPE summer program six members of the program (the "Group of Six") return to the group room after their first two hours of individually visiting patients in a major hospital in southern California. The supervisor facilitates their group disclosures about how it went in that initial exposure to people who are experiencing serious, painful life situations. The group members differ considerably in their stories.

Cynthia for example, a 52-year-old Filipino religious sister, shines with delight in reporting that all of the people she met in patient rooms were quite happy, getting along well with their medical conditions, positive in their interactions with her, and appreciative of the hospital and its caregivers. Van, a 27-year-old Vietnamese immigrant Catholic theology student tells about long conversations he's had with two patients about their emigration experiences and some Catholic perspectives on Bible passages. Jane, a 37-year-old Presbyterian ordination applicant and mother, stifles tears as she recounts how she has stayed mostly silent with an aging man and his dying wife. Ed, a 32-year-old former academic scientist, has spent his hours sharing perspectives on church politics with a family of three Roman Catholics like himself. Sal, a 29-year-old Mexican church musician and Buddhist convert, remains aloof as he describes physically, two patients with whom he has visited briefly. And Ben, a soon-to-be-ordained Orthodox priest cannot be clear with the group while excitedly multiplying words about his initial patient care experiences that afternoon.

For all six of them the ACPE program has suddenly become real. After a week of orientation to hospital and CPE policies, procedures, regulations, and organizational geography, they have met patients and tried to help them. They all express anxiety in one way or another, and all have touched and been touched by face to face encounter with genuinely sick and injured people. They are about to engage in a 400-hour educational experience set up to help them explore their caregiving habits, theological thinking, interpersonal skillfulness, and attitudes about human tragedy. They will soon have fundamental decisions to make about how much they will invest personally in the unique and challenging learning modalities that make up an ACPE clinical education program (Figure 1.1).

To what degree will they let themselves become an integral part of this meticulously prepared program intended to help them accelerate their learning of how to help people who are engulfed in life-changing human predicaments? Some might remain in compliance mode, doing only what will gain them academic or ecclesiastical credit for the program. Some may wade into the edges of its teeming waters, trying a few suggested new perspectives and skills. Or others can dive in and move forward towards the rich depths of transformational learning that are possible for them there. They will most certainly retain lifelong memories from choosing either of the latter two.

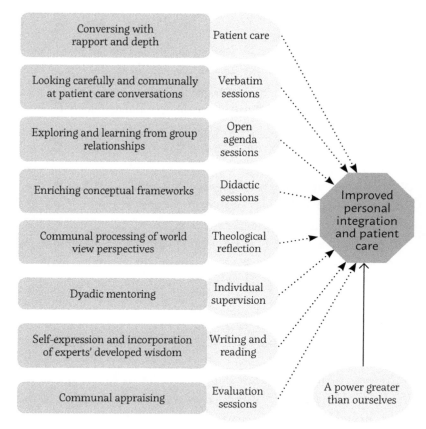

Figure 1.1 The primary methodologies of clinical pastoral education

The immediate future of these six, mostly young and all inexperienced in healthcare culture, will be a combination of the quality of the program on the one hand, and the investment each will make in its handful of primary learning modalities on the other. What are the learning program elements and the positive changes that can occur to group members if they choose to vigorously and courageously engage them? The first learning modality they have just tasted, that will jostle them towards new ways of being, is the experience of focusing new learning on direct patient care.

Direct patient care

When we urge a theological student to get clinical experience outside his lecture room and his chapel, to visit the sick, the insane, the prisons and the alms houses, it is because we want him [sic] to practice his theology where it is most needed, i.e., in personal contact with individuals in trouble.

DR. RICHARD CABOT (1925, SURVEY GRAPHIC)[1]

When intern spiritual caregivers walk into an ACPE program, they can be assured that there are people not far away caught in struggles with personal pain. They can expect to be emotionally moved by patients' stories, to feel some inadequacy about their unique predicaments and puzzled by some of their interactions with the neophyte group member as a potential trusted spiritual caregiver. At best, it won't be a comfortable program. The intern will benefit from knowing that discomfort is a pervasive aspect of healthcare and that their own level of anxiety will best be met with tolerance, courage, resilience—and learning.

New group members are assigned immediately to care spiritually for a defined group of real people in real pain. That aspect of the program alone constitutes what many group members later consider to be its best and most challenging aspect. For many it is the first opportunity to connect with the ACPE program as an adventure rather than a quest. Allow yourself to start a new adventure with every patient, rather than meet that moment as a piece of the quest for seminary credit or filling a denominational requirement. The first learning from direct care of people happens best through a combination of the caregiving itself on the one hand, and processing conversations with peers and an experienced mentor on the other. But a great deal is learned by some fledgling chaplains through patient contact alone. Such actual caregiving experience is

---

1   Reprinted in Cabot, R. (1926) *Adventures on the Borderland of Ethics*, pp.1–22. New York: Harper and Brothers.

likely to have the following life-shaping effects on group members' personalities and subsequent lives.

STRIVING FOR EMPATHIC CONVEYANCE AND COMPASSIONATE CARE

Cynthia, the first member of the Group of Six described in the introductory comments above, began to learn from peer and patient feedback that she brings way too much cheeriness to patients on initial contact. She generates in them a need to please her, to keep interaction with her light and enjoyably social. She has yet to learn how to engage people with an open stance to their situation, whatever that may be. She will likely need to drop longstanding habits of engaging people gregariously over her years as a saleswoman, teacher, member of a religious order, a favored daughter, and a convivial friend.

Spiritual caregiving is different from all of those. It requires an ability to connect with people with a view to what they are feeling inside, how they are experiencing their moments alone while languishing at times in their predicament. Cynthia feels compassion for people sometimes but has never learned to hew that vague altruistic sense into a receptive approach that establishes rapport with most patients. Her CPE group members may be key to her recognizing the changes that need to happen within herself that allow greater depth in her engagement of people in need. She has begun to pursue an art that is never done perfectly, but that often helps people with difficulties that nothing else that is human can reach.

Compassion is described by Ellen R. Cohen, MSW, President of the Schwartz Rounds organization, as combining the *feeling* elements of empathy with the *active helping* inclinations of sympathy.[2] People in need beckon forth from people a natural human tendency towards altruism in a compassion that a new group member may never have

---

2   Ellen R. Cohen, MSW, Schwartz Rounds current president, in her plenary session address in Houston at the Association of Professional Chaplains national conference, May 2017.

recognized inside her before. Being charged with the spiritual care of all kinds of people in that situation of need catalyzes a vague empathic sense into efforts to care for them, in any way we can find. We are compelled to tolerate the awkwardness of failure in those difficult conversations, and to continue to make that caring effort better. Direct patient care also fertilizes motivation for investment in learning new ways of caring that we had never known before. One of the first new competencies ACPE group members struggle with, is effectively *conveying empathy,* actively showing people that we "get" them in the present moment, at least on some significant level. That motivates the new learning from the educational elements of the program (see Figure 1.1).

LINGERING (INTERACTIONAL WAITING)

One of the specific skills of conveying empathy, a key though elusive component of personal listening, is reining in the natural tendency to "do" something to help. A simple skill catalyzed by interacting with patients is intentional waiting. A sensitive student learns from direct patient care, often with the help of peer and professional supervision, the skill of *interpersonal lingering.*

The most important five to eight seconds in spiritual caregiving are those of intentional silence at key moments of the dialogue. If the caregiver waits long enough, it gives the patient time to consider what to say next, and almost invariably leads to deepening or broadening of the conversation. Reducing the use of questions as interventions generally adds to that skill. Questions can over-direct the conversation, tending to keep its content narrow and the asker in control. Deftly conveying empathy allows what is happening inside the patient to further come forth, often only in the second or third topic of the dialogue. Learning the skill of lingering—waiting after a significant patient disclosure—is key to establishing rapport, and is taught informally and unintentionally by patients to caregivers who can become astute in observing their own patient interactions.

Jane, from the Group of Six, had already learned to linger, or was naturally gifted with it. She had that capacity to wait clearly validated by the group a few days later in the program. The man with the dying wife felt it that first day.

GROWING ALTRUISTIC FOCUS

Most all of us humans possess a natural altruistic bent that motivates us to want to be of some use to others. Managing the tension between altruism and self-care constitutes a major piece of being an effective caregiver. Idealistic pouring out of ourselves to others can move towards burnout and compassion fatigue. But the opposite, preoccupation with ourselves, even in well-meaning anxious reticence or hyperverbal reflexive chatting, almost precludes care of others. Direct patient care in hospitals pushes us to negotiate the tension between those two poles.

Initial experiences of patient spiritual care tweak many group members' natural human curiosity. Run amok, that tendency to get in on another's personal misery can miss the notion of care completely in what is colloquially known as busy-body gossip. But a measure of interpersonal curiosity combined with altruistic intentions fuels deepening conversations and real personal listening, as opposed to diagnostic listening, which is focused on finding out what's wrong from the caregiver's point of view rather than what is rumbling inside the patient himself. The skill of showing genuine, not feigned, caring interest in the patient's situation, current feelings, interpersonal concerns, and attitudes to their situation can grow with experience and persistent effort. A significant measure of it, however, is needed for even the most basic level of establishing caregiving rapport.

Three of the Group of Six had been unable to organize themselves to do anything active in their patient conversations. Showing interest in the internal experiences of patients—interest that is real, astute and kind—is a basic skill that deepens care. Combining altruistic curiosity with quiet and empathic presence was yet to be learned by any of them.

RE-FOCUSING

In the rapidity with which patient conversations can unfold, it is easy for any caregiver, even experienced ones, to miss cues patients give unconsciously that significant issues lurk beneath their social or compliant patterns of conversation. You may become used to noticing a few seconds later that you have missed the best opportunity to connect with a patient more deeply. That nagging frustration motivates learning to be a bit "quicker on the draw" in responding humanly to your perceptions.

Re-focusing is a simple skill that improves conversations substantially when important clues have been missed. In other words, the ability to recognize having missed hints of latent concerns and then return to them seconds or minutes later helps "find" patients emotionally more often. This skill is especially useful given the ways in which we humans habitually protect ourselves from the vulnerability that follows our making substantive disclosures. If you don't hear a patient's clue the first time, she will most likely repeat it, offering you a second or even third chance to hear and respond to it. Failing that, you still may be able to nimbly redirect the conversation minutes or even a day later, to significant possible spiritual needs that have been unconsciously, partially disclosed. A common patient conversation may go like this, for example:

> *Patient*: Yes, I have a little house next to the Edison school. Yeah, my wife used to teach there and died a few months ago, so I like hearing the kids giggle, yell and even scream. My own kids...
>
> *Chaplain (moments later)*: Say, wait a minute. Did you say a few minutes ago that your wife died recently?

There arrives a new chance to hear the grief of a relatively new widower that may be just under the surface and perched ready to be heard.

HUMAN-TO-HUMAN ATTITUDE

Some group members arrive for an ACPE program with an already developed style of engaging people with an "I'm OK, you're OK" attitude.[3] But others surprise themselves when talking to a patient by finding that they have longstanding habits of subtle paternalism, well-intended moralism and benevolent but incessant teaching. Some find that they habitually convey an impression that they know more, are healthier, and possess superior wisdom for virtually anyone they meet. Having the edges of that mostly unconscious attitude knocked off by the confusion of one patient, or the intractable painfulness of the life of another, is likely to either discourage their budding spiritual caregiver career or propel them to improve their attitude towards the basic value of care for all people. Excessive preoccupation with people of the culture and dogma of a single religious group can impede that growth.

That was what initially challenged Ed, the Catholic scientist on that first day. He noticed on his own that he highly favored talking with Catholic patients, because that is what he had been educated for in the seminary. What about the other patients of varying religious backgrounds, or none, some of whom, from a purely human perspective, may have needed real care?

INTERPERSONAL SUPPORT AND ITS LIMITATIONS

Supportive responses to people in difficulty are roughly what children need for comfort, and what adults often need when in crisis or even when faced with other less dramatic needs. Assurance and reassurance, by someone familiar with the strange milieu that surrounds you, someone who neither exaggerates nor minimizes the situation, feels like a solid foothold on a mountain cliff. It allows people to feel less alone and possibly find their own best self-care response to the situation. Those would-be caregivers who were not comforted much themselves as children may have a therapeutic

---

3   Harris, T. (1969) 'The Four Life Positions.' In *I'm OK, You're OK.* New York: Harper and Row.

task ahead of them to become ready to serve as caregivers who are called to simply support others many times per day. Supporting others constitutes a great portion of spiritual care work, especially when depth of interaction cannot be achieved. In struggling to say something supportive, a new student can find themselves speechless. However, platitudes quickly feel hollow. Patient care can show a person how difficult it can be to effectively support.

All of the Group of Six had in some way been supportive of the patients and families they had visited. But five had not used any skills to deepen the conversations beyond the social. There is far more to care of the human spirit than support.

COMPASSIONATE NORMALIZING

Exaggeration in situations of crisis is common. People in troubling situations tend to either fearfully exaggerate their predicament on the one hand, or they minimize it so it seems like nothing on the other. The ability to bring a realistic perspective to a person who has been unconsciously using hyperbole to describe their situation can be termed normalizing, showing that person that the situation is rather common and they don't need to feel embarrassed, sick, or unusually challenged by it. Doing so without paternalism, however, or otherwise generating bad feelings about themselves in a patient, may take some skill acquisition. This is another challenge presented by direct patient care.

HONORING LIMITATIONS

Beginning ACPE group members quickly encounter patient situations that are beyond their ability to address. But the budding caregiver may not naturally know how to draw the line between what they can do and what they ought not to address beyond being a temporary supporter. Patients can shock new caregivers and unintentionally teach them how to recognize and honor their own limitations. Exaggerations of one's own responsibilities and competencies can easily produce disastrous situations. Having a handle on one's own limitations and knowing how and when to refer a patient to other caregivers, stands as a basic competency for the authorization to function even as an intern spiritual caregiver.

Easy as it seems to maintain physical, emotional, and role boundaries while visiting with hospital patients, it can challenge and confuse new group members. Figure 1.2 illustrates three areas of a caregiving relationship continuum, from under-involvement, to over-involvement, with the zone of the helpful in between. New group members commonly enter the continuum from the left, until they develop some skills for deepening their relationships with patients beyond the social and supportive. At some point you will doff the customary relating with which you have been traversing life and caregiving, as you begin to deepen relationships centered on the primary concerns of patients and work to elicit those. You are then more often entering the zone of the helpful.

Under-involved	Zone of helpfulness	Over-involved
Keeping emotional distance with conversations that are superficial, remain social, or become pedantic, patronizing, or ritualized		Exploitive or even abusive, physically, socially, emotionally, financially, sexually; flirtatious; indulgent

Figure 1.2 Continuum of caregiving relationships

One issue of over-involvement illustrates how one can enter it even with the best of intentions. Some patients will attract you. When you feel that and recognize that it may be mutual, it is time to know the boundary of caregiving. If you give a person for whom you are charged to care an inclination that you may be interested in a romantic or sexual relationship with him or her, then you have already crossed the line of unethical behavior. You'd best seek consultation with another professional and terminate the relationship. Perhaps that seems harsh and unnecessary. It isn't. Hospitalized people are in a vulnerable situation, in bed, in a semi-public situation. What is appropriate and ethical in much of our daily life interactions is not always so in a caregiving setting. In this scenario exploitation could be imminent. ACPE programs include extensive orientation sessions prior to patient contact by group members. Take advantage of them.

These nine initial learnings begin for inexperienced caregivers a path towards the personal formation of a caregiving identity; they become people who can quickly gain initial rapport with almost any other human being. They motivate a budding practitioner to reach a professional caregiving style beyond the social, the diagnostic, and the tolerant. Such skills will not come easily. Direct patient care beckons an interested student into this new identity and prods him on to discover more. Skills begin forming through dedicated and persistent engagement of the other learning modalities described below. The most central of these in CPE is the group processing of written verbatim reports of caregiving conversations.

The verbatim [4] : writing and presenting

Knowing your own darkness is the best method for dealing with the darknesses of other people.

C.G. JUNG[5]

ACPE group members learn in three very different ways: *alone*, in reflection, reading, and writing; in *dyads* with the supervisor and informal conversations with peers, chaplains, and colleagues; and *communally*, in the group setting. The first group modality is the

---

4   The word verbatim is an adjective turned into a noun by common usage of CPE students and, eventually, supervisors. It refers to the written report of a spiritual care conversation to be used for the purpose of looking carefully at it under individual or group supervision.

5   Jung, C.G. (1973) Letter to Kendrig B. Cully, September 25, 1931. In G. Adler, A. Jaffe and R. Hull (eds) *Letters of C.G. Jung Vol.1, 1906–1950*. Princeton, NJ: Princeton University Press, p.237.

communal processing of members' written reports of their caregiving conversations, which has come to be known simply as "the verbatim."

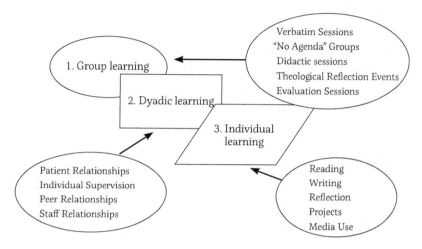

Figure 1.3 Three types of ACPE learning

The culture that develops around that classic ACPE learning modality finds no equal in professional preparation for caregiving. CPE started with case studies, and then evolved into first emphasizing verbatim studies. The small group of caregivers dedicated to openly and extensively processing verbatim reports of real patient conversations challenges every group member and promotes learning for every peer. The repeated 75 minutes[6] of engaging peers and a supervisor constitutes the primary work of ACPE groups. It lays bare the core of group members' personalities, shows them the communication habits that keep their patient conversations superficial, and by its very nature challenges them to further develop their self-awareness, helping skills, caregiving style, and professional competence.

---

6   Some ACPE programs have moved to an hour or even 45 minutes for each verbatim. The author believes that often the most valuable depth of learning happens after the first hour and reducing that time below 75 minutes misses a great deal of the self-explorative depth.

The "verbatim" or clinical session remains the core focus of CPE.[7] It is legendary among seminary students, parish clergy, and any academic field education professors who have ever had a conversation about CPE. A unique experiential learning modality developed over time by several early clinical pastoral educators, it was first emphasized as the core of CPE by Russell Dicks at Massachusetts General Hospital in the 1920s, during the time that CPE was being born.[8] It seriously challenges the caregiving practice of every CPE group member who authentically participates.

All else in CPE revolves around group verbatim sessions that bring the peer members together as effectively as possible to look closely at a single spiritual care effort made previously by one of them. That close, group operation sets CPE apart from all other disciplines. The facilitated collaborative inspection that fends off inevitable interpersonal conflict in the service of exploring what was accomplished in the pastoral contact constitutes a modality that is almost always beneficial and sometimes unforgettable. No other profession uses it as significantly in a group setting for training their professionals.

---

7   See Figure 1.4. The verbatim can reasonably be seen as educationally central among the primary ACPE program learning modalities, being augmented by the others. Administratively and theologically, patient care would be considered to be central. The others are essential but secondary to them in ACPE programs.

8   Several books that chronicle the origin and history of the clinical ministry movement are: 1) Joan Hemenway (1996) *Inside the Circle: A Historical and Practical Inquiry Concerning Process Groups in Clinical Pastoral Education*. Atlanta: Journal of Pastoral Care Publications; 2) Charles E. Hall (1992) *Head and Heart: The Story of the Clinical Pastoral Education Movement*. Journal of Pastoral Care Publications; 3) Stephen King (2207) *Trust the Process: A History of Clinical Pastoral Education as Theological Education*. Lanham, MD: University Press of America; and 4) Edward E. Thornton (1970) *Professional Education for Ministry: A History of Clinical Pastoral Education*. Nashville, TN: Abingdon Press.

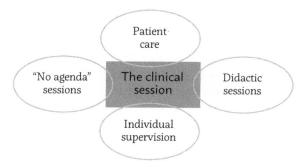

Figure 1.4 Centrality of the verbatim/case study
session among the ACPE learning modalities

The verbatim session is not a discussion. It does not facilitate merely talking *about* the spiritual care interaction written in the verbatim. It directly *engages* the verbatim presenter from start to finish. That person is the focus of almost all the group interaction. It requires engagement,[9] a kind of interaction of direct focus on one group member with a stake in the issue at hand, especially including their genuine current emotions as shown by tone of voice and non-verbal behavior. It generally begins with a look at what they say in the session about what they remember that they said in the patient conversation on which they are reporting. The group culture of authenticity is most crucial here.

---

9   The word "discuss" derives from the Latin *dis-* "apart" + *quatere* "to shake," or
     figuratively to examine by shaking apart, debate, or argument. "Engage" on the other
     hand is from Old French *engagier*, i.e. *en* meaning in, with "bind" (by promise, oath, or
     pledge). Engage better represents the interpersonal interaction in a verbatim seminar
     in the sense that group members encounter one another's emotions as well as their
     thinking and memories about the spiritual care conversation being presented for
     processing. "Discuss" has come to mean a conversation that focuses mostly on the
     cognitive aspects of a topic.

The general purpose of the group processing[10] of a verbatim is to develop self-awareness of group members and spiritual care skills. Richness in this aspect of the program constitutes the group's primary work and can be said to be the most memorable and fruitful component of CPE. Learning to function well in group verbatim sessions optimizes benefit from CPE and pays off during a caregiving career.

The verbatim has been tweaked, refined and adapted by most all CPE supervisors as they develop their style of working with students. In all ACPE programs it is used in peer group sessions and sometimes in individual supervision with each student privately as well. This most powerful feedback mill begins with one group member's initiative in preparing a written account of a single spiritual care conversation.

WRITING A VERBATIM

The CPE program schedule will designate the dates on which students are assigned to present verbatim reports for group processing, generally in some rotation sequence that shares the presentation responsibilities relatively equally among them. The curriculum requires that all group members make presentations; nobody remains uninvolved in producing the data for group learning. All are thus at least minimally vulnerable to the critique of their peers. The "presenter" for a given session has agreed to provide typed copies of a written report that captures the conversation of a spiritual care event as accurately (verbatim) as possible for all members. Writing a verbatim presents the first challenge of this learning modality.

Recording the data of a patient conversation for a verbatim report presents the first difficulty. We're not socially prepared to keep track of each voice and each statement made by both parties

---

10 The term "processing" here refers to close examination of the dynamics of a conversation, in particular the emotional happenings, reactions, responses, and inner-sensations involved in the interaction, as objectively and collaboratively as possible. This can be done in a facilitated group setting or individually between one student and a skilled clinical supervisor.

in a conversation. Nobody is used to that kind of careful attention and prolonged memory. As a presenter, your responsibility is to record the conversation as accurately as possible yet not become preoccupied with its exactness. This will become easier with practice. But as we will see below, self-awareness grows exponentially for most students immediately upon taking up the practice of writing verbatim reports. Remembering what was said, as accurately as possible, is a skill that grows quickly with repetition. Since the pre-conscious mind wanes in a very short time, it is important to write down the actual words spoken in the conversation, as soon as possible after the patient encounter. Sketch it out even before exiting from the immediate area if possible, though of course not within view of the patient. You will sometimes be amazed at what you write as compared to your conscious memory later as you process that conversation with peers or a supervisor.

All ACPE programs suggest a locally adapted format for the report, to standardize as much as possible the data presented by students who vary considerably from one another. The formats differ with supervisor, program, level of CPE, and time positioning in a residency year. The key elements, however, are always about the same. They have been found to generate lively feedback and engagement during the group processing time, of preferably at least 75 minutes.[11] The list of these basic, universal elements—in whatever configuration they are included in the verbatim format—serve as a roadmap for the presenter in preparing the document. The standard elements include: an introduction to the patient that describes what the verbatim writer knew about the patient before they met; a "focus point" articulating what the presenter hopes to address first in processing this conversation; a reasonably full verbatim account of what each person said in the conversation; comments about

---

[11]   Some programs have reduced the time for verbatim processing, but the classic configuration included ample time for the presenter to be led into a deep self-explorative foray into unconscious dynamics crucial to the quality of the patient conversation.

what the presenter felt and observed as each part of the interaction unfolds, including emotions observed in both patient and caregiver themselves; reflections on the conversation as seen in the typed version; and reflections on various aspects of the conversation as focused by the verbatim form for that particular CPE unit and its unique themes.

An example of one format for verbatim presentation is included in the Appendix.

The following list gives some tips on how to develop the report for optimal group processing:

1. Immediately after the conversation, sit down and, without reflection, record notes about what was said by both you and the patient. The pre-conscious memory lasts less than two days. It is important to get your freshest recollections about the actual dialogue.

2. Since you may have recorded notes about several of your care conversations, choose one about which you either feel quite good because of its success; one over which you continue to ruminate because of vague feelings or its vexing elements; or one that prompted a relevant question you have about how you dealt with the patient's concerns or unique features.

3. Stifle any inclinations you may have to alter the actual dialogue with what you *wish* had been said.

4. After typing the verbatim dialogue portion, write an introduction that describes whatever you know that you think is pertinent about the patient, particularly what you knew about that person before you met them, and basic facts about them as a person and as a patient. You can include why you visited the patient, what they were doing as you entered the room, why you visited with them, and any details you noticed about their surroundings and their visual self-presentation.

5. Write a brief statement, one sentence preferably, about what is, after reflection, your primary concern to be responded to first by the peer group. Called a "focus point" in most verbatim formats, it provides a starting point for the group processing.

6. Include as much detail as you can about what happened during the conversation. Include what was said by anyone else in the conversation such as other clinicians or family members present.

7. Also include what you noticed about the patient's voice tones, behavior clues, and especially facial expressions. Much of spiritual care takes place in the countless expressions of the 43 muscles of the face. Record how anything about the person evoked emotions in you. This too gets easier as you practice writing verbatim reports.

8. After writing and then typing the verbatim portion of the report, sit and reflect on it quietly. Then address the other areas of reflection required by the verbatim format of your program. These vary greatly by supervisor, level of CPE, and curriculum themes of that specific unit of CPE.

9. Finally come up with a creative title that in some way intuitively conveys the character of the entire verbatim project.

When the group is assembled and the scheduled time for your verbatim presentation has arrived, you have a copy for each group member and the supervisor. You are the one who begins the group exploration.

PRESENTING A GROUP VERBATIM

When it is time to be the presenter of verbatim material for group processing, take initial charge of the group. Your peers will likely be either socializing or nervously chatting. It is your responsibility to bring focus to the group onto your verbatim document. How you conduct yourself during the session will determine to a great degree what you learn and how valuable it will be for your practice of spiritual care as well as your personal relationships. Here are some suggestions about how to benefit as the primary focus of this highly personal group exercise.

Let the group experience affect you. Defensiveness on your part is a given. After all, closely examining your exact care interventions is the sole purpose of a 75-minute small group of peers. You will feel like defending your tack in the patient conversation, your basic competence as a person and a caregiver, and maybe even your personal worth. And you will need to do so to some degree. The group members were not observing the patient conversation directly when it occurred so there is no way for them to fully experience it as you did, and only your memories of what was said are on the paper, not the exact words that were spoken, nor all the feelings felt. All interpersonal conversations carry far more communication data than can be represented in writing.

Still, when your verbatim report is the subject of the group interaction, let the group affect you, repeatedly. The educational experience relies on your engaging with significant authenticity of disclosing what you are currently aware of from the conversation and your responses to probing questions, validating comments, and critique brought by the group. Monitor your attitude as much as possible. This is done optimally not by staying aware of it, which is quite impossible, but rather by tuning into it occasionally as you spontaneously respond to group queries and feedback. To what degree are you feeling misunderstood by the group as a whole? No group apprehending of the care conversation being processed will be completely accurate. A considerable amount of trust that there is enough understanding of it to be valuable is essential on your part. Even if several of them say that your face is green, take out a mirror before escalating your defensiveness to an impermeable fortress.

One way to conceptualize the optimal verbatim session attitude is to find a place on a continuum between the watertight stubborn and the sickeningly acquiescent. Find the middle ground that will let you seriously consider all group points of view offered while not being willing to "sell the farm" and accept all feedback perspectives as accurate. Acknowledge what seems reasonably possible to be true about you as a person and as a caregiver, and offer a better perspective on whatever seems to you at the time to be quite inaccurate. No matter what the outcome of this session you will most likely come away with a sharper cognizance of yourself in conversations with patients and peers than you had when you entered that group consultation room that day.

Reduce your aversion for crying during the group interaction. Let your feelings overcome you if they are strong. Tears ordinarily only signal that your very soul has been touched in some significant way. That may well be transforming for some aspect of your caregiving. Poise is invaluable is some situations, and even in verbatim sessions to some degree. But so is strong expression and confrontation in the best sense of the word as "standing face to face willing to be honest." Strengthening that capacity will show itself as invaluable in spiritual care conversations with patients with strong feelings.

There is likely to be conflict of some sort and at some point when you present a verbatim. You may learn something about your typical response to conflict in what follows. If you ordinarily tend to skew your response to conflict by fighting, acquiescing, hiding, obfuscating, flatly denying, blaming, ignoring, or otherwise avoiding conflict then you probably will in this context too. You may be surprised at the levels of anger kindled in you by critique that seems exaggerated and off target. Real education often means leaving behind an old way of seeing yourself, and even adopting a new aspect of improved self-perception. Strive for courageous openness and trust the group to find you.

It is likely that you will find yourself saying things that you never planned or intended to say during a verbatim session focused on you. When we are thus learning "in the moment" we are venturing beyond our old selves. The longer you can persist in this explorative interaction the more likely you will emerge the richer for growing awareness. Use of concepts from practical personality theories such as the Johari Window, the Myers Briggs Type Indicator, the Enneagram, or Transactional Analysis may be used to assist you in embracing the long-hidden parts of yourself that can be revealed in this kind of group session.

THE INDIVIDUAL VERBATIM SESSION

In some programs the supervisor makes regular use of processing students' verbatim reports while meeting with them in individual supervision. Other supervisors will do so only prescriptively, when it is suggested to deal with a specific issue pertinent to a given student. This practice then becomes part of what could be called the "dyadic learning" or "learning in pairs" aspect of CPE. Here are some tips for maximum benefit.

1. Write a verbatim reporting on a patient visit that either baffles you, felt vexing at the time, or evaded insight during your private reflection on it.

2. Follow the focusing input and queries of the supervisor, responding to it even if it feels extraneous at first.

3. Allow yourself to make associations with events or people in your past who come to your mind in response to questions and invitations of the supervisor

4. Include in your immediate reflections, references to peer group members that come to your mind, the presence of whom you believe would impede your sharing the case in the group, and any other reason you prefer to share this one outside of the group context.

The verbatim II: participating in a peer's presentation

At bottom and just in the most important things, we are utterly alone, and for one person to be able to advise or even help another, a lot must happen, a lot must go well, a whole constellation of things must come right in order once to succeed.

RAINER MARIA RILKE, LETTERS TO A YOUNG POET[12]

A great deal of learning in CPE derives from taking active part in the group processing of another member's verbatim session. The primary work of this session is the generating of feedback to the presenter and engaging them about their thoughts, feelings, memories, and motivations conveyed in the written report and their current comments and responses about them. You do well to resolve to learn what you can by this communal experience.

Here are some actions that can optimize that learning, including what to do at the beginning, during, near the end, and after the meeting. The presenter here will be called the "chaplain" and the person receiving care, the "patient."

- In most ACPE programs, the written report is read aloud or dramatized at the beginning of the session. During that time place yourself in the situation of the patient as it is described in the report. Try to identify with the patient in the personal aspects of their medical predicament. What is it like to be them? How might you respond to the chaplain if you were them?

- Next, examine the "focus point" identified by the presenter. It is the part of the conversation with which the presenter suggests the group start the processing. What is the presenter

---

12 Rilke, R.M. (2011) '5 Viareggio Near Pisa April 1903.' In *Letters to a Young Poet*, trans. Charlie Louth. New York: Penguin Books. First published posthumously in *Briefe an einen jungen Dichter* (Leipzig: Insel Verlag, 1929).

looking for? And what might the presenter be doing unconsciously in that focus point? Do you sense anything less than genuine about it? If so, decide whether to verbally note that now, to consider it data to be referred to later, or to ignore it altogether. That is a decision to be made many times during a single verbatim presentation. There is so much contained in that one conversation that not nearly everything can be brought to the attention of the group.

- While the document is being read, you may also benefit from labeling each written chaplain comment with one of four types of pastoral response as described by Howard Clinebell in *Basic Types of Pastoral Care* (Clinebell 1984),[13] a classic of pastoral care literature first published in 1966. His view—that a spiritual caregiver can only respond to a patient in four ways—is still useful these several decades later in analyzing any verbatim report. According to Clinebell, a spiritual caregiver can 1) *ask a question* to gather information or foster further patient disclosure; 2) *offer support* in a positive, encouraging statement; 3) *suggest an interpretation* that offers insight into what is happening or has happened to the patient; or 4) *reflect* what the patient is conveying emotionally or experiencing at this moment. All these interventions have their place and are highly valuable at specific times. In the careful listening promoted by ACPE programs, however, the latter remains the most difficult and often the most deeply connecting of chaplain to patient. This simple analytical project early in the verbatim session can offer great clues to the care offered by the chaplain in the written report.

- You will likely find yourself analyzing and evaluating as the verbatim is read, forming impressions as to what is

---

13 Clinebell, H.J. (1984) *Basic Types of Pastoral Care and Counseling: Resources for the Ministry of Healing and Growth*, pp.65–68. Nashville: Abingdon Press. First published in 1966.

happening in both the patient and the chaplain. That is the purpose of the verbatim: to understand what happened inside each of them during the original conversation, and then how the chaplain is presenting and learning during this session. Making explicit what seems to have gone well, what might be improved, and what the presenter may benefit from looking at more closely, constitutes the group learning process.

- As you and the group engage the presenter about the patient conversation, there is opportunity to use concepts that refer to dynamics seen to recur frequently in verbatim processing. You can benefit from gaining a practical understanding of several of these, which are adopted from psychoanalysis to have their own similar meanings that can be clearly visible in the group dynamics. These common concepts can find realistic understanding in the intense dynamics of verbatim sessions.[14] Sorting out these dynamics can bring great insight into caregiving conversations and the processing that happens in verbatim sessions. Learning more about them and learning to recognize them in yourself or a peer, adds a great deal to ACPE learning. Three of these concepts are identification, transference, and projection.[15]

---

14   Others that are quite common are intellectualizing, rationalizing, obfuscating, displacement, and the minimizing of denial.

15   In ACPE programs, *identification* refers to an empathic understanding of another person, an association with that person of a feeling similarity. As in Alcoholics Anonymous the term, "I can relate to that" signals the experience of identifying with another in a way that leaves all others behind temporarily as a remarkable perceived bond in one's mind, that sees the other as "like me" in some significant way.

  Transference as a concept has been variously interpreted. In CPE groups it means the unconscious distortion of a group member's emotions relative to a peer or patient who somehow resembles, in some emotional way, the group member's parent or other childhood person of importance to them. Whatever word is used for this phenomenon, it is a concept that, so far, is indispensable in the analysis of group members' peer and patient relationships.

  Projection refers to a more specific inner process in which a group member perceives their own characteristics to be in another person, without seeing them in themselves as vividly first. Group feedback can be helpful in a group member separating themselves from their own projections, to see themselves and others more clearly as they appear to others.

- For example, look for *identification*—the experience of perceiving another as highly similar to yourself, even an extension of yourself—as if you were them. This is almost universal in some way, and can be confusing and even disruptive if there is *over*-identification, which will be unconscious at first, and may remain so if not commented on by an observer. It can be seen in highly favoring a group member, treating them preferentially and finding it more difficult with them than others to be objective and risk feedback. It can also highlight feedback when they offer it or agree with it when offered by others.

- The common experience of *transference* is also frequently observable clearly among group members in verbatim processing. It shows itself most often by feelings, positive or negative, that seem to an observer as exaggerated and of an intensity that would not seem to fit the situation. Countertransference, as it occurs in a spiritual care person about a patient, is commonly seen when pointed out by a group that sees its distortion in a presenter's emotions in a verbatim session. Working through stark experiences of transference and countertransference can be high points of an entire CPE program experience.

- *Projection* is a related but different dynamic, in which one person seems to see in another person an aspect of themselves that may not actually be present to any great degree in the other. Does that patient really find you as attractive as you think? Or are you mostly finding them attractive?

- Learning to partially trust your *intuition* in verbatim processing can be delicate, only achieved through actual trial, checking out your quick grasp of something by verbalizing it tentatively a few times in the group. You can start it in a given instance with something like, "Can I check something out with you?" knowing that the other person may not be aware of what you are intuiting at all. The verbatim group is a good setting in which to work on this intuitive use, however, so use it with courage and etiquette. Use of metaphor, story, wisdom quote, song phrases, and even pointedly relevant jokes in gaining insight into a patient or patient conversation depend on allowing intuition to surface.

- You can engage the presenter in a host of different ways, based on your observations of the written account and the group dynamics that have transpired so far. Offering validation, for example, asserts that you like something the presenter did in the patient conversation. It differs from flattery and polite, ritualized support, in that it is measured, authentic, and devoid of exaggeration or patterned verbiage. We learn from our successes, and every verbatim session flows more smoothly with some validation first, and then again unpredictably throughout the processing.

- *Critique* on the other hand, offers a perspective that differs from what the presenter has shown. It suggests a better view of a dynamic, skill, or personal characteristic that presumably could improve the presenter's caregiving. It can be highly susceptible to causing conflict however. Group members implicitly agree to be willing to critique the presenter in the interest of them seeing something they are not seeing, or seeing it differently from how they have previously. Offering critique is a primary agreement of the group members relative to one another in the program, and some level of competence in it is an expected ACPE outcome of Level I programs. Risk it and learn to do it effectively.

- Another engagement skill is actual caring for the presenter by showing them that you comprehend on some level what they are feeling at any given time, with affect that communicates care in the moment. Beginning to care for your peers and learn from your patients is often an indication of advanced learning in ACPE programs.

Several of these group interventions during a verbatim session will be enhanced by strategizing. While there are times when a spontaneous response fits the situation, there are others in which crafting the words of an intervention to minimize the defensiveness of the presenter works much better in maintaining the learning situation. Strategizing in your mind before critiquing, interpreting or confronting has a chance of better being heard than edgy, spontaneous reacting, even if the latter feels more exhilarating.

Reflecting after a verbatim session

After a verbatim session, group or individual, there is benefit yet to come. Whether you are the presenter or a peer participant, you can benefit from a fresh activity such as taking a brief walk or sitting quietly to reflect on the rich and perhaps unsettling feelings that linger from the starkness and intensity of the group interaction.

As a peer presenter you can well allow yourself to think about the following:

- What were the most emotional moments of the group interaction? At what points did you feel the most deeply? What words stand out that preceded that moment? Who said them? How do you feel now about that person? Write a few sentences about them.

- What was this group trying to say to you overall? How would you summarize the salient messages to you during that hour?

As a peer group member, after rich group processing of a verbatim, your reflections can center on a few simple questions:

- What is the general value for spiritual care of the central issue that confronted the presenter?

- Where have I seen that issue in myself, about myself, or in my care of people?

- How has my impression of the presenter been enhanced, deepened, or expanded by this session?

Early in the evolution of CPE the intricate dynamics of verbatim processing were shown to require another kind of group session as a necessary companion modality.[16] Relationships among group members get tense since group verbatim sessions immediately become highly personal. When a group of human beings looks closely at one another's professional conversations, dynamics among those members invariably become catalyzed and splintered into conflict on the one hand and collusion on the other, through hurt, annoyance, intimidation, covert alliances, and discouraged evasions (hiding). At those times the rigorous objectivity needed for educationally fruitful verbatim processing quickly gives way to distortions, defensiveness, and sullen avoidances. A different kind of group session is needed: the open agenda group, to keep the group culture relatively free of prejudices that grow. That type of session, a well-known staple of ACPE programs, is the subject of the next section.

---

16   The purposes and use of the open agenda group were the subject of much discussion and published thought over the formational years of CPE. See King, S.C. (2007) *Trust the Process: A History of Clinical Pastoral Education as Theological Education.* Lanham, MD: University Press of America, pp.65–67.

The open agenda group

It ain't what you don't know that gets you into trouble.
It's what you know for sure that just ain't so.

AUTHOR UNKNOWN[17]

The most storied aspect of CPE is the open agenda or interpersonal relations group (IPR). Known by several other names as it is conducted variously by different programs, as an intensive and extensive group project, it is a unique educational milieu not found anywhere else across professional disciplines. It carries several purposes, based on the overall objective of ACPE programs—to prepare people for care of the human spirit in difficult life situations. The open agenda group fosters caregiver interpersonal resilience for care in raw, starkly distressing crisis care situations; it serves as an arena for processing the intra-group conflicts generated by verbatim presentations and other peer presentations; it provides a training ground for group members to care for one another and learn from attempts to do so; it becomes a space for group members to work experientially on their learning goals; and it helps group members develop skills in facilitating groups in their caregiving work for the rest of their careers.

One key to the open agenda group is the pervasive practice of strongly suppressing mere discussion and easy socializing in the group. The insistence on authentic communication begins in the very first session and is maintained throughout the program, through the final evaluation session. Spiritual care conversations are not social engagements, and neither are the group interactions intended to examine them. The IPR group lends itself well to developing accuracy of perception and practicality of conceptualizing, to forming new identities and skills of engaging in the special ways various patients

---

17   Misattributed to Mark Twain, conveyed through a colorful story in Ralph Keys' (1993) *Nice Guys Finish Seventh: False Phrases, Spurious Sayings, and Familiar Misquotations.* New York: Harper Collins, pp.73–74.

need, and for sharing spiritual perspectives with interdisciplinary teams.

All ACPE groups provide some brief instruction on cognitive frameworks for understanding people, the intricacies of care and the nature of transformational learning. While these vary considerably across programs, they all open ways to learn about oneself more deeply than previous experiences have done. One of those, created in 1955 and still used briefly by many ACPE programs is called the Johari Window.[18] Dividing the human personality into four sections, or "windows," it gives group members a way to think about and observe the processes of self-disclosure in a small group setting. The value of direct feedback and talking seriously about yourself is especially highlighted in terms of reducing the "hidden," "blind," and "unknown" areas while further developing the "open" aspect of your personality. The underlying theory is that as your peers become more familiar with your history, thinking, and immediate emotional experience, the openness of your self-disclosure flourishes. Feedback then becomes increasingly valuable.

There is no solid preparation for engaging in an ongoing IPR group process. Like entering patient hospital rooms, prisoner cells, and psychiatric common areas to engage people who are hurting, the IPR never becomes completely comfortable. But nobody ought to enter ACPE programs expecting to find a comfortable place. Becoming a quality caregiver of the human spirit is always jolting to a degree, as old ways of interacting and seeing relationships fall away, and new ones are created, almost with every new patient contact.

Experience with many ACPE groups has resulted in some suggestions about how to get the most out of an IPR group experience. Here are some common ones.

---

18   The Johari window model was devised by American psychologists Joseph Luft and Harry Ingham in 1955, while researching group dynamics at the University of California, Los Angeles. The model was first published in the Proceedings of the Western Training Laboratory in Group Development by UCLA Extension Office in 1955, and was later expanded by Joseph Luft.

RISK ENGAGING CONFLICT

A goal of the group is to help members face, engage, describe, and even embrace interpersonal conflict. More will be said about this in Part II. ACPE group members eventually notice the deep differences, personality styles, histories, attitudes, and strong values that tend to separate them. These differences will not go away. They are a part of life. They teach us to embrace scary diversity in order to benefit from its richness. Great lifelong learnings and transformational changes occur in ACPE peer groups due to the diversity that supervisors typically seek to include in the group makeup. A group member can sometimes learn in silence from the differences of other members' ways of seeing and meeting the world. But overt conflict is very likely to arise and you can learn even more from engaging with the conflict and then receiving feedback on how you did so. Trying to avoid all the group conflict would miss a major value of ACPE programs.

TRUST, THE PROCESS, THE SUPERVISOR, AND EVENTUALLY YOURSELF

Know that trust of a group is never complete or perfect. There is no completely safe place to be a person where a flow of honest feedback is a major objective. Especially if you seriously do not trust a peer or two, opening your observations, opinions, and needs can be a most difficult task. There is a phrase in ACPE group history, "Trust the process[19]". In this context it means overcome your trepidations about *individual members* and trust the group *as a whole*. Start your disclosure, issue, or confrontation anyway, and let the group contain whatever may give substance to your fears. This kind of trust in a supervised group grows confidence born of competence and even interpersonal excellence. Trust me.

---

19   This is the title of Stephen King's book on CPE history (2007) *Trust the Process: A History of Clinical Pastoral Education as Theological Education.* Lanham, MD: University Press of America.

TAKE INITIATIVE

We all make observations in a group. Actively bringing select ones forward remains an art. In the silences during an IPR group, search yourself for what you think needs to be a topic in the group interaction, and find the courage and the best words to speak your thoughts and feelings about it. That develops interpersonal courage and initiative to a more prominent place in your personality and is much of what makes an IPR rich, or even adequately effective.

LEARN TO CONFRONT, INCORPORATE THAT ART

Set your mind to learn how to confront, in the best sense of the word. From the Latin through French, *com* "with, together" plus *frontem* "forehead," it means "to stand face to face willing to be honest."[20] When you have a serious concern, bringing it out in an interpersonal context surrounded by colleagues who can join and offer direct feedback can be one of the most powerful educational events in preparation for colleagueship in a profession. Confrontation is a true art, and many addicts would not be alive today without it being done well in treatment therapy groups. It is equally valuable in ACPE learning groups.

USE CONSULTATION AND REQUEST IT, EVENTUALLY WITH RELATIVE EASE

From the Latin *con*, "with," and *sultare* "to strike," this concept perhaps best captures the goal of ACPE experience: to learn how to consult with peers frequently and easily about your practice of spiritual care. It is what you are doing together in verbatim sessions, and what is often needed when questions arise in your professional caregiving later on. It saves many a career when difficulties and dilemmas present themselves at least several times in nearly all careers. Dynamically it amounts to opening up the details of a gnarly interpersonal situation to a few peers you trust as dedicated

---

20 "Facing one another in defiance or hostility" did not enter the meaning until the late sixteenth century.

to your profession and your wellbeing. Opening yourself in seeking consultation, and being patiently wise when somebody is seeking it from you, grows maturity as a professional caregiver.

VALIDATE CAREFULLY, PRECISELY, AND GENEROUSLY

Many of us grew up in families in which little actual validation of our worth and our uniqueness was available. Learning to say what you like in another person—their work, their thinking, aspects of their group engagement, and heaven forbid, even their self-presentation and appearance—must be distinguished from flattery and reflexive polite encouragement. Flattery is manipulative, sometimes even with the best of intentions. Polite support falls flat as not substantive or genuine. Validation is a gift which is given in the moment, and can be unforgettably valuable. The validation among peers in an IPR group can differ considerably from that in a verbatim group. In IPR it is about current dynamics, observable to all other group members. That makes it even more personal than the validation of caregiving performance more characteristic of verbatim sessions.

NOTICE SUB-GROUPS

A significant group theory used in some ACPE programs features the way in which mini-alliances within a small group ebb and flow with issues and group events.[21] That theory uses such sub-groups to further the processes of self-disclosure, self-awareness, and interactional growth of group members. Other programs attend variously to the inevitable formation of sub-groups to either use them in processing dynamics or to keep them in check from over-influencing the flow of feedback among the group members. Group members are naturally drawn to some peers more than others, and those affinities ebb and flow over time. A person new to ACPE programs will notice that identifications, alliances, mutual protectiveness, and outright collusions waft freely in a supervised small learning group and that

---

21   Agazarian, Y.M. (2004) *Systems-Centered Therapy for Groups.* London: Karnac Books.

sometimes it will be helpful or even necessary to point them out. At the very least they are sometimes powerful dynamics that can either contribute to or impede the open flow of direct feedback for which these groups are conducted.

FINALLY, KEEP AN ATTITUDE OF ADVENTURE
AS OFTEN AND AS LONG AS YOU CAN.

Your perspective is invaluable to group process but not infallible. Learning to honor the uniqueness of your experience, while not enshrining it as always accurate, moves you far ahead in benefitting from IPR. It takes you into places you have never been and shows you things you have never seen. There is treasure there. Some of the things you have known for sure just ain't so.

The didactic input group session

We must think differently, look at things in a different way. Peace requires a world of new concepts, new definitions.

YITZHAK RABIN[22]

The integrative character of CPE always includes some cognitive input to fuel insight into people and people-helping processes. Clinical education based in direct observation and interpersonal experience tends to be the right hand of academic education's left-handed cognitive and research orientation. But ACPE programs are not only clinical. They are designed to be integrative. In the immersion in intense action/reflection processes, ACPE program curricula include the presentation and discussion of some conceptual material led by professional experts who are excited about what they do in their caregiving roles and enjoy teaching about it. These group meetings are generally referred to as didactic sessions.

---

22   Yitzhak Rabin, US Congressional Record, House, vol. 156, Pt.5, Page 6028, April 21, 2010.

In spiritual care of patients, we seldom if ever know exactly what we are doing since it is unfolding in front of us, inside us, and along with us. But conceptual frameworks that have previously consolidated disparate ideas inside us lend some structure to our work of continually improving our understanding of people and caring processes.

Clinical educators conducting ACPE programs generally decide on a theme or two for each unit of CPE. They then look for interdisciplinary didactic presenters of topics associated with those themes. Supervisors give some thought to what this present intern or resident group may benefit from just now, and then inject topics that are likely to fit the need. The format is simple and standard in ACPE programs. It includes 30–40 minutes of input delivered in practical terms that can be interrupted by the group members' questions as agreed upon at the start. The input is followed by 20–30 minutes of the group members "picking the brains" of the presenter, focusing their queries on how the input is useful from a spiritual care perspective. It can be illustrated by graphics drawn in the moment, or by brief and clear handouts that clinch the main points of the presentation. It is often closed with suggestions of what to read or where to go to continue expanding on or deepening group members' understanding of the concepts.

The following are some examples of the didactic topic lists of one recently conducted ACPE program:[23] spiritual assessment; drinking problems in the general hospital; chemical dependency and its recovery; moral injury in returning military veterans; compassion fatigue; transgender inclusiveness in the workplace; palliative approaches and end-of-life considerations in adults with eating disorders; the evolution of palliative care; the grief of children; communicating difficult news; understanding the ostomy process; from detached concern to empathy; humanizing medical practice;

---

23   Providence Portland Medical Center, Portland Oregon, Sandra Walker, certified educator.

evaluating non-verbal behavior in patients with dementia; and what happens in a code blue from a medical perspective.

The possible topics are endless, limited only by the availability of experienced, enthusiastic presenters. Enter each of these sessions expecting that they will be practically effective in adding to your spiritual care conceptual and caregiving skill competence. Pay attention, take a few notes, ask good questions, and thank the presenter.

Individual supervision

Our chief want in life is somebody who shall make us do what we can.
                                                    RALPH WALDO EMERSON[24]

Investing an hour in one-on-one meetings with the program certified educator adds a dyadic component to the group and individual learning CPE methods that can consolidate benefits of the program and address problems in learning along the way. When a group member is able to maximize use of this modality—traditionally called individual clinical supervision—the result can be a pivotal mentoring relationship that forms a permanent piece of one's career. This relationship allows the group member to bring almost any agenda to confidential discussion. It lets the group member decide what to focus on week to week, generally write a few sentences about it, and accomplish several endeavors during the program. In that curriculum component a student can: carefully form and monitor the evolution of prescriptive goals; obtain insight into complicated peer relationships; process problems with specific patients; explore relevant aspects of personal history not yet ripe for group discussion; clarify conceptual aspects of caring being emphasized by the program; lodge the first level of a complaint about the supervisor

---

24   Emerson, R.W. (2004) *The Conduct of Life: Considerations by the Way.* In Packer B., J.E. Slater and D.E. Wilson (eds) *The Collected Works of Ralph Waldo Emerson,* vol. six. Cambridge, MA and London: Belknap Press, p.145.

or program; and address a host of other private matters affecting the transformational learning process.

The agenda for these individual supervisor conferences (ISCs) lies almost entirely in the group member's hands. What that IC brings to initiate a session best begins with an emotion that person has about the intended issue and proceeds with dialogue that mixes feelings and thinking towards integration of a concern and forming of a new perspective. It often opens other issues as well, not intended to be part of the student's original agenda but emergent during the interaction. Many supervisors require a written summary of the group member's inner experience that week or another written statement that serves to bring initial focus to the supervisory hour. The written statement or oral issue presented, well chosen by the IC, is some event, peer relationship, patient relationship, theological concept, or memory that has struck her as relevant and that to some degree preoccupied her mind that week.

Trust in this supervisory relationship is even more crucial than trust in the group for making the entire program beneficial. If the level of that trust is low, it is still possible to benefit from the program. A last-ditch effort to form a quality learning alliance with the certified educator consists of raising the issue you see that inhibits your openness to them, and seeking a direct conversation about it. Lodging a complaint if the CPE program staff's ethics, the program quality, or the educator's competence[25] are seriously lacking, is a last resort. This is so because individual supervision is a key component of CPE. Having had a professional, objective and knowledgeable person involved intimately in your thinking, feeling, and functioning around the intricacies of caregiving, even for an initial three months of clinical education, brings a maturity and

---

25   The ACPE Standards that are current can be found on the ACPE website, ACPE.edu, currently at www.manula.com/manuals/acpe/acpe-manuals/2016/en/topic/200-standards-complaints. A complaint can be about the professional ethics of the CPE staff (Ethics Standards 100s), the CPE program quality (Accreditation Standards 300s) or the supervisor's professional competence (Certification Standards 400).

confidence to one's practice that can't be equaled by other aspects of the program.

Theological reflection sessions

Theological reflection...is not just "thinking about." It is an attempt "to open up and penetrate matters which are present but hidden." The group's reaction is...not just dispassionate thinking clearly separated from the event. The event has claimed involvement and demanded response.

JOHN PATTON[26]

The term theology does not fit well with some spiritual caregivers who practice a religious tradition other than Christian. But ACPE programs are still accredited with the commitment to include reflection on transcendence—the Divine, the Ultimate Other, the Higher or Greater Power for example, as part of their explorations of spiritual care relationships. In one way or another, perspectives on transcendence as a major component of helping relationships and one's caregiving practice will be brought to the group by any ACPE program, as well as by patients' drastic situations. This clinical type of learning is often traditionally called by its Hebrew/Christian reference: practical theological education. As part of that, what is commonly called theological reflection is facilitated in several ways in the group and individually.

- theological perspective paragraphs in written verbatim reports

- group processing of sermons or homilies in preaching or religious teaching seminars

---

26 Patton, J.H. (1995) *From Ministry to Theology*. Eugene, OR: Wipf and Stock Publishers, p.96, first published by the *Journal of Pastoral Care* (1995). Patton is partially quoting here, Edward Farley (1975) *Ecclesial Man*. Philadelphia: Fortress Press, pp.71–72.

- drawing attention to theological perspectives spontaneously during verbatim, open agenda, or didactic sessions

- processing extensive written presentations of the group members' pastoral theology, pastoral psychology, or religious development in one-day retreat settings

- theological reflection seminars in which patient conversations are presented with the understanding that the focus will be on theological perspectives and concepts, while actively suppressing the kind of interpersonal examination and critique of the conversation characteristic of verbatim sessions.

Focusing communally on what group members believe they can stand behind as their own theology of caregiving brings a confidence to caregiving practice. It invariably challenges a group member's theological thinking in ways that promote further reflection, deeper reading, further academic theology, or later consultation with a trusted mentor or academic theologian who is familiar with practical theology and how it develops in a practitioner's life. The new group member will again need a certain kind of courage to risk their thinking and critique of theological traditions and their own experience, imagination, and comfortable conceptualizations and language to allow this method to affect and educate them to stronger confidence amidst contexts of the obviously uncontrollable such as hospitals.

Processed written evaluation

The effort really to see and really to represent is no idle business in face of the constant force that makes for muddlement.

HENRY JAMES[27]

---

27   Blackmur, R.P. (1983) *Studies in Henry James.* New York: New Directions Publishing Corporation, p.31.

Evaluating a person or an incident in writing is comprised of three major projects, all interpersonally perilous. The first is finding the courage to manifest your own evaluative opinion or perspective clearly to other people. There you need to boldly *reveal your values and perspectives*, making them vulnerable to serious discourse and even debate. The second is *finding the words* to accurately and gracefully describe what you are seeing and experiencing. Words matter, especially when you are evaluating something or somebody important to you. And the third is daring to *write that down for all to see*, perhaps forever. ACPE programs use methods that require those three together in several ways, all challenging group members to prepare themselves for accurately describing and appraising patients and colleagues in a professional caregiving career.

As a major component of the ACPE program efforts to promote personal and professional integration, processing group members' own prescribed writing in the group context stands as a unique and powerful learning modality. Group members are urged by the CPE culture to divest themselves of dualistic frameworks of understanding of people, as for example "unsaved," "mentally ill," "deranged," "insane," "sinful," "fallen-away," or a hundred other phrases that evoke defensiveness rather than open human-to-human dialogue. They are also encouraged to learn developmental and other behavioral science frameworks to gain insight into how various minds work and hearts were formed. In addition, they are required to write evaluatively about their relationships with peers, patients, and the program itself. What they write is observed by peers and is wide open for comment or questions by them.

The group atmosphere this creates can be intimidating at first, especially to those who have been relying on academics, vague thinking about human makeup, cognitive philosophical discussions of concepts, idealized theology, uninformed opinions, pop psychology, and other generalizations for the success of their caregiving relationships.

Evaluation in ACPE programs may begin at some point in the first few program weeks as group members are facilitated to share their first impressions of one another, within the limits of what they choose to disclose. That exercise is based on the reality that patient responses to spiritual caregivers begins with the first sight and hearing of that person who enters the door of their hospital room, often without request or even invitation. How you look and what your initial personal self-presentation says to strangers is valuable background to any caregiver's early practice. Offering that feedback begins a process of learning to evaluate usefully and compassionately rather than punitively, resentfully, hostilely, or inanely. That skill will be further enhanced by requiring a similar process at mid-unit, this time in writing.

The skill of evaluating people and relationships proceeds in the written verbatim materials presented that include a section on self-evaluation of the care provided. That establishes self-evaluation as a value in the clinical learning process. On what basis does a beginning group member evaluate themselves and the relationship they had with a given patient? How will they develop their own language for that descriptive evaluation that goes beyond the use of the words "good," and "positive"? This specific description is new territory for almost everyone who engages in CPE. Developing one's own taxonomy of rich diction and creative phraseology establishes a skill which is useful for charting professional colleague relationships.

At mid-unit a common, classic practice is to ask group members to prepare by writing a clear paragraph about each peer, describing them richly in their physical appearance, communication habits, favorite words, partially observable attitudes, apparent deep values, and common overarching assumptions, such as, "women always just have to be..." or "Catholics don't really think for themselves." Students may be provided with suggestions of how to approach this project, such as describing a group member physically as if the group were to meet them at the train station having never seen them before; or to write about their communication habits, conversational patterns, underlying attitudes, sturdy values, and common assumptions of how the world is. That portion of the evaluation experience itself, even before the group meets for the mid-unit evaluation session, presents a further challenge of evaluating people in writing in ways that enhance the people's self-awareness without generating resentful responses in them. The entire process fosters shared evaluative impressions among group members, adding to their growing capacity to use accurate description rather than judgment in evaluation and to expand their awareness of how other people, including patients and hospital staff, may be seeing them.

Another common mid-program evaluation requires group members to evaluate their own goal progress and current impressions of their strengths and weaknesses as caregivers. Writing specifically about themselves is also quite new to most students. Having it commented on by peers who have come to know them is a feedback-rich context that further refines their self-awareness of how others see them. As the ego ideal is confronted by the perceptions of closely observing others, a more realistic self-impression gradually emerges. More useful and prescriptive goals for future learning can be forming just below the surface of awareness.

During the program, as a part of the curriculum, many ACPE programs will also use a writing project as material for a retreat day format, or seminar arrangement regarding a theme on which group members are required to write beforehand. For the theme pastoral theology for example, the program may require a brief, pithy written statement of one's operational theology of spiritual care. A specific retreat theme such as grief work may require writing on a real grief issue of their own experience. An authority retreat may call for writing on particular troubling events and relationships with authorities in one's life. For group members planning to apply for chaplain certification a retreat theme may be formed by preparatory writing to evaluate themselves on particular competencies for certification that strike them as possibly difficult for them. And increasingly, the written notes a group member includes in the medical record about a patient for whom they have cared, become the object of group discussion in the interest of learning how to do that better.

The standard ACPE program includes a final evaluation group experience that highlights what each group member writes in evaluation of themselves and their peers, this time with particular attention to assessing their strengths and weaknesses as caregivers. Most often the scope of that evaluation includes evaluating the supervisor and the program as well. That process pushes students to place the ACPE program experience in a realistic perspective as they walk out the door. Evaluative functions that are openly shared have a confirming effect on group members' experience and consolidate what they have learned into their self-appraisal and caregiver practice. It clarifies elements of the gifts and weaknesses that have been mentioned along the way of the program's unfolding and prepares them to be prescriptive about goals of subsequent educational endeavors, possibly including further clinical education.

This final evaluation experience generates emotionally charged interest in how these peers and this supervisor have actually seen them to be and to function during this program. The finality of this event adds dramatic importance to the entire program as group members tend to take away from it rather vivid impressions of their strengths and weaknesses as seen by a few people who have come to know them in a particularly intimate, if time-limited way.

The supervisor's final written evaluation of each group member may or not be shared in the group context, depending on that supervisor's style of leading ACPE groups. The certified educator's role is to give a professional perspective on each group member's path through the program, their addressing of the outcomes of Level I or Level II CPE, and their impressions of their educational needs going forward. Tradition includes doing this in narrative form. In the interest of reducing subjectivity of supervisors' final evaluations some have devised standard statements organized in levels that require only the assigning of a letter or a number in place of narrative descriptions. Others believe that such changes deprive students of one of the most valuable aspects of the program—comparing their own new self-awareness with that, in writing, of an experienced, astute observer and clinical caregiver who has seen them deeply, highly personally, and expansively and taken the time and care to write directly about them in a final evaluation statement. Theology school officials have commented that if the supervisor's written final evaluation does not identify a student's learning and caregiving issues, that written document is mostly useless to them as an educational and clergy authorizing tool.

Finally, what a group member writes about the program as a whole, after it is complete, also has an effect on that group member's future professional functioning. How they evaluate the program that has so shaped them as a person and as a professional shows some of their ability to bring a relatively objective and substantive perspective to helping that program to continually improve. It also moves that group member a bit out of the lab culture of CPE and more into the "real world" of seeing program staff as people to be helped and colleagues to be joined.

Some people are far more suited constitutionally for writing than others. The art of representing anything inside you on paper can be elusive and a frustrating project for many. But the value of openly and communally discussing your written representations flies high in promoting personal integration and offering a confirmation of your perceptions in the process of learning about yourself and people in general.

Creative educational methods

There is no innovation and creativity without failure, period.

BRENE BROWN[28]

---

28   Brene Brown in Suresh Mohan Semwal (2016) *Best Management Quotes*. New Delhi: Prabhat Prakashan, p.130.

Several other dynamic learning methods have been included in many ACPE programs over the past decades that successfully inject clinical learning competencies into vigorous group members. A few that have received widespread use are described below.

ROLEPLAY

On-the-spot invitations to group members to act out a specific issue or relationship event bring new perspectives boldly into focus. For example, roleplaying an initial patient conversation during the first week of a Level I program brings focus on several aspects of the "cold call" process—visiting patients who have not requested it—either calming or alerting group members to what is a quite new endeavor for many.

FISHBOWL EXERCISES

Two persons conversing, while surrounded by colleague observers, can learn and teach when they open themselves to group feedback after it. Grief work skills, confrontation abilities, and conflict resolution capacities are rapidly promoted by such sessions.

AUTHORITY OR GRIEF WORK RETREATS

A one-day session—preferably away from the ordinary group venue—in which each group member processes writing about a relationship with an authority that was more problematic than helpful, can be both educational and healing. Similarly, a retreat that focuses on skills for meeting suspected drinking problems in a general hospital, mental illness, or medical ethics cases fosters specific skills for meeting common but specialized spiritual care situations.

PRACTICUMS

A practicum is a curriculum component that combines didactic input, clinical presentations, reading, and writing on a specific set of spiritual care competencies. Examples of theme topics include all of those mentioned above.

PREACHING SEMINARS

A curriculum component that facilitates peer feedback on what a group member says publicly when intending to support a congregation of healthcare patients and staff members can be one of the most integrative of spiritual theory, conveyed empathy, and skillful care. It furthers the application of theological perspectives to caregiving in a unique way. Such a venue optimally includes current patients and family members. They can be in a chapel service, a hospital unit gathering, or a specially arranged group of invited healthcare staff members and patients for the specific purpose of giving group members feedback on their sermon or homily presentations.

READING, WRITING, AND AUDIO/VIDEO

Language is integral to all education, and certainly so in CPE. Written and oral communication is how we have learned for at least a few thousand years. Today, however, visual media plays a vivid role in integrating the various aspects of CPE programs together. A potential CPE group member can expect use of video and audio devices to highlight various aspects of their learning. Use of distance learning media is growing as well, even juxtaposed to the widely shared belief that for clinical education, an as-yet undetermined minimum of face to face, in-the-same-room interaction is at least as necessary as it is in nursing and medical education. Facilitated self-exploration cannot be minimized if depth of care has value in preparation for spiritual caregiving.

Reading takes a back seat to processing in CPE. It would be too easy for those CPE group members who are cerebral academic achievers to get lost in their bookishness as it is more comfortable than engaging with patients and peers. But reading is also always a part of CPE. It is a way to meet the best ideas of some of the great caregiver theorists and practitioners in their writings. And it contributes to the project of developing frameworks of understanding patients and the endeavor of spiritual caregiving that contributes to spiritual care identity.

What is to be read at what stage of CPE formation is a matter of consultation, collaborative decision making, and sometimes simply an assignment.

Specific prescriptive reading may be assigned by the certified educator to fit an individual group member's particular need. Foundational reading, seen as introductory for basic grounding of a new practice of spiritual care, may be required by some programs, especially for those group members who have not completed a minimum of academic theology-type education prior to the CPE program. Other formational reading is a part of most CPE programs. The question of what to read in a given unit of CPE can be answered by suggestions by staff members or the certified educator, or may be left to the student herself. Nobody can read all the writing available and there will be differences in what a specific certified educator believes is best for a given student. What is important is that every CPE participant reads something written by leaders in a professional caregiving field in their first ACPE program experience.

The sharing and discussing of what is read, in written reports or group discussion, is generally a part of the use of this modality. ACPE programs tend to fiercely guard the clinical nature of the program, however, and excessive emphasis on reading and writing can lean way too far to the cognitive aspect emphasized almost completely by academia. Reading is generally seen as a way that students can be influenced by the writing of some of the best practitioners and theorists in spiritual care traditions. There is considerable value in reflecting on the content of what is read during clinical education, then fashioning a written report and discussing it with a peer group. Written reports on one's reading emphasize the primary content themes, their relevance to spiritual care, and the ways in which they affected the reader, along with at least a bit of critique of what was read.

Writing one's own perspectives and conceptualizations is also a possible assignment in CPE. Seeing one's thinking on paper, organized for somebody else to read and critique, helps to clarify an issue and either consolidate its usefulness through integration, or lay it bare for scrutiny and change. Some ACPE programs use suggested or assigned writing to particular group members to clarify their thinking and invite new expanded consideration of a given topic that arises in the context of group or individual supervision. Mini-retreats on specific topics often include writing as part of the preparation and as catalysts to the retreat interaction.

Conclusion

Using this unique collection of special learning methods together in ACPE programs invariably fosters the development of a transformational learning culture, both intense and temporary. That culture includes several features necessary for a group member to embrace in order to profit optimally from it. In an attempt to represent that culture and do what one can to help prospective group members prepare for it, in Part II we describe several of these features and the benefits that can be gained from personally investing in that culture.

2

Embrace the Learning Culture

Learning is not attained by chance, it must be sought for with ardor and attended to with diligence.

ABIGAIL ADAMS[1]

The first group formation session of an ACPE program initiates the development of a unique culture that ends only on the final day. Embracing that culture yields results in growth of personality and caregiving functions that cannot be equaled by other types of interactional education. Well-conducted CPE so challenges its group members that virtually everyone goes away from it transformed: some for the better, some confused, and a few a bit wounded by the efforts to dissolve their resistance to learning.

---

1   Abigail Adams in a letter to John Quincy Adams, May 8, 1780. Quoted in Diamond, M. and Hopson, J. (1999) 'Learning Not by Chance: Enrichment in the Classroom.' In *Magic Trees of the Mind: How to Nurture Your Child's Intelligence, Creativity, and Healthy Emotions from Birth Through Adolescence*, p. 264. New York: Plume.

A culture can be defined as a set of guidelines, explicit and implicit, which individuals inherit as members of a particular society, and which tells them how to: view the world, experience it emotionally, and behave in it in relation to other people, supernatural forces/gods, and the natural environment.[2] CPE creates its own culture, much as churches, political assemblies, and nursing units do. If you want to optimize the benefits from it you will need to embrace that culture as temporary, professionally overseen, and historically effective in shaping quality caregivers.

Metaphorically, there are of course, varying levels of physical embracing. There is the quick ritual hug, giving lip service through politeness, etiquette, or mildly resentful compliance. There is the affectionate hug, warmly conveying appreciation and gratitude. The reconciliation embrace consolidates healing in depth from past neglect or mistreatment. And the passionate flow of sexual pleasuring with its abandonment to carnal wildness can express human love more dramatically than anything else.

The results of CPE experience vary as much. Various aspects of ACPE culture present unique challenges, all promising different potential benefits for the individual and the caregiving practice of successful group members. The primary aspects of ACPE culture and their related benefits are depicted in Figure 2.1.

---

2   Helman, C.G. (1990) Culture, Health, and Illness: An Introduction for Health Professionals. London: London Publishers, p.2.

Figure 2.1 ACPE group members are immersed in challenging and interconnected elements of a unique learning culture

Expectations of authenticity

Spiritual care of pained people cannot afford much thoughtless verbosity, pedantic instruction, interrogational questioning, unnecessary self-reference, or comfortable socializing. Accordingly, from the very first group session, ACPE group members will be challenged to speak clearly, directly, and as openly as possible to one another. That expectation is often communicated initially in the group by inviting the peer group members to talk seriously about themselves in extended self-introductions. As much self-disclosure as each person can freely muster will be included, regarding previous geography, educational and work history, original and current family makeup and ethnicity, religious development and affiliations, and current interests and involvements.

Patterns of communication that fall short of some level of congruence of emotion, cognition, and behavior are likely to be openly described or critiqued in direct feedback at any time in the CPE culture. The typical restraining of stark openness with everyday congeniality that we mostly practice in society and even in our family interchanges is suppressed during the group time of clinical education in the service of preparing group members for the patient conversations that often need to be brief, pointed, and quickly substantive. In ACPE program culture a participant gains a level of self-expectation of interpersonal authenticity that will color their subsequent spiritual care and colleague relationships.

In the group sharing of their first patient experience among the Group of Six for example, Cynthia's habits of communication emerged as hyper-extroverted, rosy over-sharing that almost immediately annoyed two other group members who remained politely quiet about it for that first week. In the initial interpersonal relations group, however, one of them interrupted Cynthia's sanguine pedantry with a simple question: "Excuse me, but why did you think it was important to tell us that now?" As Cynthia picked up other clues about her normal communication pattern, in individual supervision and the group, she withdrew into silence much of the time, entering the group interaction only with pointed comments. She was already accepting this new milieu as powerfully propelling her into self-reflection about her effect on other people. Her voice was almost immediately weightier among her peers. She was learning that in a clinical education group it is best to refuse to say much that you don't really mean during group time.

Unfolding process

ACPE programs fiercely maintain the process nature of education. That means that the programs each unfold in their own way with a congruent continuation of one interpersonal event and issue into another. Structure is crucial but not sufficient.[3] The primary emphasis is on learning from experience as it unfolds and on making space and time to explore what is happening in the present moment, inside

---

3   Bruner, J.S. (1977) *The Process of Education* (2nd edn). Cambridge, MA: Harvard University Press, pp.17–32. First published in 1960. Accessed on 18/12/2017 at http://edci770.pbworks.com/w/file/fetch/45494576/Bruner_Processes_of_Education.pdf

each learner and among them. This aspect of ACPE programs can be subverted in many ways and it is the supervisor's role to prevent those subversions. A few common ways to impede the process quality of the group interaction include: over-use of structure; excessive instructing; avoidance of group conflict; lapsing into extensive cognitive discussions; skirmishing over dogma and other ideological differences; externalizing to generalizations about global happenings outside the group; scapegoating one group member to unconsciously shield the others from engagement; excessive intellectualizing, in group interaction as well as in reading and research assignments; and prolonged debate over the correctness of anything at all. All of these amount to group resistance[4] in which supervisors sometimes collude temporarily until they recognize the dynamic.

New group members are usually accustomed to more academic cultures on the one hand, and training cultures on the other, the former emphasizing cognition, and the latter emphasizing skills and activity.[5] CPE at its best is both training and education, as it integrates brief instructional understanding, caregiving practice of practical skills, and emotional awareness of interpersonal dynamics. That can take a new group member a bit of time and adjustment to negotiate and make useful for learning.

Immediate relational processing

Much of the benefit of ACPE programs for group members accrues through the ease and frequency of what is called processing. In the CPE context that word means looking carefully, calmly, communally,

---

4   This unfortunate education term, as used in CPE, means ordinary patterns of communication and behavior that inhibit a student's exposure to what is new in the learning context. It is considered to be unconscious until made conscious by being noted verbally by a peer or supervisor. It is commonly misunderstood to be intentional obstruction of what the supervisor wants, or the program curriculum requires.

5   The difference between education and training can best be described by the proverbial father who received a letter from his daughter's school saying that the class was soon beginning sex education. He quipped, "If it had said sex training, I would have gone straight to the police!"

and as objectively as possible, at specific interactions between two or more of the group members. The immediacy of this unique culture element helps group members become increasingly aware of the effect their words and behavior have on people, which is especially relevant in CPE as preparation for and enhancement of spiritual care.

Processing generally includes taking a few moments—in a sense, creating space—to explore the feelings, thinking, observations, and intuitive responses of people present to a specific interpersonal interaction that they all have observed. The practice of calling for the processing of an interaction at almost any time creates a cultural element of ubiquitous self-observation and alertness to others' behavior that increases overall self-awareness, circumspection, and skills to work through troubling interactions that occur in their personal and professional relationships.

Focus on emotions

ACPE groups are known for the focus on emotions that characterizes them. That is because spiritual care is mostly about feelings and their underlying concerns, values, attitudes, and dashed habitual assumptions. In these groups emotions are seen as constantly emanating from perceptions and the heart of our experience. All of the joy and all of the pain of human existence lie in that teeming bed of compelling senses, impulses, and trepidations that gives us a unique window on what we see, hear, and even smell. CPE groups at their best are cohesive group members helping one another become more familiar with what they feel at any given moment, as preparation for focusing on the feelings of people they are trying to help.

Learning to distinguish the various levels of anger, from annoyance to rage, as distinct from the prior piercing sensation of hurt, and their consequent shades of fear-led avoidances, comes from embracing a temporary lab of persistent interpersonal interest in one another's emotional experience. That makes the famous CPE question, "How do you feel about that?" expressed in a hundred different ways, the key one of the entire CPE experience. Along with "What do you make of that?" as an invitation to think anew about something immediately relevant, it repeatedly brings one to greater awareness of one's own feeling life that has remained only partially in awareness until that point. Not that anyone is ever perfectly aware of this inherently mysterious emotional aspect of humanity. But helping one another become more thoroughly aware of and willing to share the flow of what is affecting one emotionally in the immediate situation may be the greatest gift of CPE peers to one another.

Feeling frustrated in the third week of the program, David mentioned, half seriously, wishing for a list of feelings so he could ponder the "How do you feel" question before answering it. A peer mentioned the "feelings wheel" that can easily be found in many forms on the internet. The supervisor responded with the list of six universal feelings that are often found on the walls of addiction treatment facilities to help with tuning in to what a given person is feeling in present time. They include the most neglected experience of *hurt*; *fears* that result from past hurts and potential harmful impending events; some form on the continuum of *anger* that generally accompanies hurt; the down or discouraged experience of *sadness*; the *guilt or shame* resulting from regrets and inadequacy; and the only positive one, being *glad* or joyful. The beginning CPE group member does well to expect to be invited frequently to shift gears from cognition and reflexive vocalizations, to awareness of the emotional strata always flowing between and among us humans.

Personal openness

Openness as a personal trait is as compelling as any other personal characteristic. Extending beyond honesty, openness shares easily the unique stories, self-observations, attitudes, values, perspectives, moods, and assumptions that make up the inimitable character of a personality. Sharing one particular incidence of any of these seems to evoke a natural inclination to share more, in oneself and in those around. Honesty refers to truthfulness; openness refers to richness of disclosure. Such sharing, the essence of intimacy, unites people almost immediately. Only inexperience, or negative previous experience, deters or defers this normal tendency to connect with others by communicating aspects of their inner world with other souls.

Spontaneous sharing of what one never consciously intended to say produces new awareness of what is inside oneself – what we did not know we thought, perceived, felt, or leaned towards. That mass of complexity includes unconscious biases, hidden resentments, brilliant or quirky ideas, lost memories, astute perceptions of others, and unique ways of seeing our world. As this more spontaneous sharing pulls out of us what we didn't know was in there, we increase our awareness of ourselves, including our avoidances of clearly seeing other people as they are, in their glorious complexity and unseen depth. We are becoming finer, more egalitarian caregivers.

Such simple and fitting graphic devices as the Johari Window make this process understandable and practical for facilitating the process of disclosure and growing self-awareness among group members. While it seems "touchy feely" to the overly cognitive, those who embrace the group sharing process become almost immediately more aware of themselves and invested in the process. They won't ever be the same. They are discarding their previous marooning in narrow habits and patterns that allow them little access to other people's depths. They begin on a path of growing human development that can stall sometimes, but never really ends.

For some, the inertia of marked introversion impedes the open sharing; for others it is the hyperverbal extroverted social patter that needs to descend into areas closer to the soul. Most all of us, however, will need to overcome some reticence to the radical openness of flourishing CPE.

During the first week of CPE, beginning to share with a group of peers how one was affected by initial efforts to meet and care for patients' spiritual needs, catalyzes the enkindling of this open sharing process.

Empathic engagement

The focus on emotions in CPE groups naturally promotes empathic engagements among group members. As characteristically compassionate people, group members are inclined to engage the perceived emotions of one another. When a group member notices hints of annoyance in a peer, for example, they will likely draw attention to that, inviting further disclosure of what it is that their peer isn't liking. Whether subtly hidden or overtly menacing, the resultant culture of care among group members, including the processing of conflicts, encourages further open disclosure and the development of skills to promote empathic engagement with patients.

The astute perceptions of one another shared in a committed peer group consolidate into an ability to listen far more carefully. Healthcare clinicians, principally physicians and nurses, are trained to listen very closely to match up their observations, patient disclosures, and frameworks of medical understanding or nursing practice in the process of diagnosis and patient management. Chaplains, however, need to listen in a completely different way, to allow surfacing of what is going on in the patient when focused questions aren't being asked.

There could be several words for listening, given this patient encounter difference as well as how we listen differently to colleagues and still differently to spouses. Personal listening, as distinct from diagnostic listening, results in patients finding inside themselves the broader concerns of their lives at this particular moment, allowing an entirely different kind of care. By enhancing their interpersonal skills, ACPE group members are becoming better personal listeners through persistent empathic engagement with one another. Personal listening is certainly done at times by medical and nursing caregivers, but it is quite brief and rather rare, and then generally seen as outside the normal practice of those professions.

Availability of support

A component of CPE's collaborative group culture is a natural tendency for human beings to support one another. The ideal pastoral role as envisioned by society likely includes that it will be positive, edifying, and broadly supportive of those involved. The etymology of the term "support" indicates it came from seafarers needing a port in a storm. The emotional strata of healthcare culture can feel to group members like an inner whirling gale, making a small group of easily listening ACPE peers such a seaport for relief from vexing patients and staff. This supportive net usually survives conflicts and confrontations that arise among the group members. Reliance on the availability of support among peer group members not only buoys the spirit in difficult work, but it increases one's trust in oneself, and it confirms one's confidence in regularly navigating the frequently jostling waters of healthcare culture.

Supportive comments as patient care interventions amount to a great percentage of what chaplains can say to patients in the crisis aspects of caregiving. They are often just what patients and family members need. Sorting over-support as a superficial style of chaplaincy from prescriptive, supportive, and active personal presence remains a basic learning of early CPE. The supportive atmosphere of a vibrant CPE group assists the learning of both supportive and more substantive care.

In his first group verbatim report, it became clear that Ben's wife had experienced a devastating miscarriage in her first pregnancy and it had seriously affected Ben. It laid inside him as a mostly ungrieved loss, since he never got the interpersonal context that it needed to emerge due to his acquiescence and dedication to his wife's greater need. The verbatim content and process led to him openly and substantively sharing his experience of that time of loss and he visibly showed emotion during the group interaction. Jane, as the only other married person in the group, served as a key in the group's support of Ben. Her ability to identify with the intricacies of romantic intimacy and differences in how partners can grieve helped Ben find words for personal support that could then be amplified by other group members. All of them were motivated by an unspoken, underlying assumption that group members would be intentionally supportive whenever a group member needed it. Though that commitment would be limited, of course, it had definitely been established and would be counted on to a significant degree in the subsequent group life.

Communal validation

Support is one thing; validation is another. It is not too reductionist to say that CPE was invented to get clergy persons' feedback on how they were affecting the people they were attempting to serve. About half of that feedback likely is validation—hearing that what one says and does in caregiving is valuable by another person's estimation. The etymology of the term validation again injects some insight into its essential meaning. The Latin *validus* means "strong, effective, powerful, active." It evolved to mean "sufficiently supported by facts or authority, well grounded." In group interaction, validation refers to how one person's behavior is made valid by the corroboration of other group members. Validation brings out the value of something: an importance of its worth that was already there but partially hidden. It celebrates the goodness of that thing, expanding it in the process. Some of the personal validations received in CPE live forever after.

Validation differs from flattery, which exaggerates people's positive aspects to gain favor with them. Solid validation emerges only with astute and accurate observation of people's finest characteristics, their shining traits, efforts, skills, accomplishments, choices, or actions. It finds words that carry a bit of enthusiasm for the goodness of that person. For Christians and many other humans, validation is an expression of the gospel, that all people everywhere are of marvelous value, and it exemplifies that belief in this moment, in this instance, with this person.

For the excessively entitled, critique may be more prescriptive than validation.

Radical acceptance

ACPE culture includes a group member impression that underlies all its other aspects, especially validation and support. There develops a sense that an individual group member is uniquely accepted for themselves, and even related to with an underlying delight in them, regardless of their past mistakes, failures, and neglect of responsibilities. The certified educator conveys this attitude particularly in individual supervision but also at times in the group interaction. Validation and support are mostly episodic, available, and offered at times of success and struggle. Radical acceptance underlies those and is more. Everyone involved remains human, of course, so this acceptance has its limits such as the need to expel a group member for good reason. But even then, such a dismissal is devoid of moralism, and maintains the essential value and personal beauty of every person. The expelled one is seen as needing another form of care or education rather than as bad, deviant, ignorant, or obstreperous. The Buddhist reverence for every living being and the Islamic commitment to submission to how Allah influences the world here dovetail with the Christian gospel of the Divine treasuring all her creatures.

Flow of critique

We learn from our successes as they confirm our worth and our competence. But along with validation of our finer points and better moments, we also learn—often even more pointedly albeit less comfortably—from our weaknesses, our failures, and our mistakes, especially those we don't see on our own. When one enters the intense temporary lab of CPE one is well advised to know that one will be expected to offer timely critique to one's peers and to effectively use critique received from them. This is why two of the nine expected outcomes of Level I CPE in the ACPE Standards are focused on offering and receiving critique.

The act of finding words for saying what you don't like about a peer's caregiving work, or indeed about their personal characteristics such as style of approachability, their communication habits, their attitudes, and their treatment of their other peers, is often the most difficult aspect of CPE for nice people who aspire to be professional caregivers. The most common quip about resisting learning how to offer useful and timely critique is, "I just don't want to hurt other people."

Indeed, the first commitment of the Hippocratic Oath is *primum non nocere*, or "first of all, don't make the patient worse." But clinicians often need to do things that cause patients pain to stem destructive processes that are progressing within them. Lancing that boil, giving that shot, setting that bone, all stand as common examples. Spiritual caregivers too sometimes need to confront, albeit without moralism or patronizing, the self-defeating and obstructive behavior of patients and family members. The ability to offer critique is one of the keys to success in CPE, both for oneself and for one's peers. How else would a group member recognize what their best next learning goals should be, other than by accepting, reflecting on, and making use of critique?

It wasn't until final evaluations that Sal looked stunned as he heard several members of the Group of Six point out that he hadn't named a single personal or professional weakness in his written materials. He was speechless when he could not then even think of one then, after several moments of reflection. Hints of that feedback had been available to him during the weeks of the program, but only now, as the entire group allied to feed back the effects on them of his aristocratic bearing, his kind and gentle preoccupation with his own experience, and the impression of specialness that he seems to cultivate around him, did he recognize it. The two aspects of CPE culture—a mixed flow of giving critique and receiving it—combine to create the rare atmosphere that can vastly improve self-awareness of group members.

Attention to conflict

Conflict remains a given in healthcare culture. There is conflict in clinicians' disagreements with one another, conflict within patients who simply don't want what is happening to them medically, and conflict in patients' self-destructive disabilities and philosophies of life such as dependent personalities, lethal self-neglect, and addiction oppositional moods. In this crisis-laden milieu, latent conflict frequently becomes overt. To work in places where people are hurting and getting help that they also resist, being cared for by highly sophisticated and busy professionals, a caregiver needs skills of conflict tolerance and conflict resolution, especially as many chaplains and other helpers commonly function as conflict avoidant and overly nice spiritual caregivers.

CPE culture maintains an openness to hear, notice, address, and process conflicts that erupt within the group and in external conflicts brought to the group by its members who are struggling with them in their patient care and in their lives. The basic skills of dealing effectively with conflict are learned from this culture that embraces conflicts as learning opportunities.

It is often the annoyances among peers that signal conflicts that are ripening for processing, in order to learn from them. Anger on any level is disdained by a good percentage of neophyte caregivers. So even recognizing latent conflict can be a stretch for them. Even acknowledging aggravation by a peer and addressing one's role in contributing to it amounts to an exponential leap ahead in learning to meet conflict as an unavoidable experience in caregiving.

In individual supervision Cynthia had talked rather freely about an incident in which she had been "dissed" by a peer. In the program's second week, she had arrived in a patient's room in response to an emergency code in a hospital unit that had been assigned to another group member. She responded to the call simply to learn about the chaplain's role in such codes. After observing the interdisciplinary team (IDT) care event to its end, she heard some patronizing instruction from the peer and heard him say directly to her, "I prefer that you not come to my unit for these codes." Cynthia responded compliantly and politely but became aware that she had felt dismissed, disrespected, and even mildly insulted. She was encouraged by the supervisor, but not pressed, to address the event in IPR group. She said she would consider it and then decided not to do so. At mid-unit evaluations that peer was the only peer Cynthia identified as one she would not want to work with or work for. A group member openly wondered why.

In the processing of the event that followed, Cynthia still never mentioned the insulting event. She did, however, acknowledge unpleasant feelings about the peer, and agreed that they would fall somewhere on the continuum of anger, far closer to annoyance than rage. Comparing the Myers Briggs types of these to group members, ESFP and INTJ, suggests one reason for the quick conflict between them. The two and the group identified some of the similarities between them as habitually thinking of themselves as quite intelligent and more used to cognitive perspectives than affective ones. Their life experiences as an extroverted female Navy leader and an intuitive male academic scientist were referred to, and they gained considerable insight into one another's personalities. They did not become friends and likely never will. But the entire group had opportunity to see the anatomy of colleague conflicts that quite commonly erupt in work situations, how they can exist covert for long periods of time, and how they can be ameliorated to a useful degree by group facilitation.

Ambiguity and paradox

Healthcare culture is filled with ambiguity and paradox. In spite of the efforts of science-based helping disciplines to keep things rational, controlled, scheduled, uniform, standardized, and evidence based, the entire "system of systems" that constitute a hospital teems with the uncontrollable. The "something beyond us all" always has its way eventually, and often in this very moment. Nobody can accurately and comprehensively predict what that "way" will be. No solid world view seems to fit the situation of infant death. Alcoholics "kill themselves on the installment plan" on the one hand and become the most responsible, sensitive citizens on the other. Random evolutionary unfolding pervades. Medicine and nursing care continue to progress despite over-management, exploitation, and flagrant waste in this mass of paradox between celebrating healing when it happens and accepting the outcome when it doesn't.

The CPE culture is congruent with that mix of scientific progress on the one hand and perpetually ambiguous outcomes on the other. CPE groups constantly increase their grasp of the behavioral science attempts to understand and conceptualize about what is sensually validated among them. And they do so while boldly facing the inherent mystery that is the reality of every person. A peer group member, for example, says one thing and finds themselves in mystified tears for doing the opposite, repeatedly. Concepts that fit now in one situation tomorrow ring hollow in a similar one. What seems firmly true in one's individual reflections, limps and pales in group discussion. Exhilaration over establishing rapport with one difficult patient gives way to confusion after discouraging failure with three others in one afternoon.

Whatever spiritual philosophy, theology, or world view emerges from group members' experience with patients and outcomes in healthcare culture will need to include the impossibility of ever figuring it all out.

Group cohesion

This almost palpable force that draws the group together with one another, nags them internally to be present at every session. They all come to recognize this pull to not miss what may be happening in the group when they are absent. Like the natural inclinations to go home, to gather for social engagements, and to show up for family events, group cohesion drives ACPE group members to be together for personal growth benefits even when those benefits remain as yet unnamed and some unrecognized.

Experiencing solid cohesion in a group for a time lets group members know what a close group is really like, to which they can compare other groups in caregiving practice over their careers. In addition, it shows them many behaviors that impinge against development of group cohesion, that are collectively called (unfortunately), resistance.[6] Recognizing group dynamics and individual dynamics in the small group context prepares a person for all kinds of group, committee, and project work in other communal contexts later on.

Van, a 27-year-old Vietnamese immigrant of ten years, the youngest of the Group of Six and a candidate for ordination as a Catholic priest in a few years, was proud of his Bachelor's degree in psychology. From the beginning he brought unique questions to the group interaction, stayed to himself in free time and kept an obvious eye frequently on what the supervisor was doing. His primary stated goal was to overcome a cultural aversion he called an almost overwhelming fear of dead and dying people. By mid-unit he had made great progress on that goal after nearly fainting on his first time in a morgue. When it came time for mid-unit evaluations,

---

6   The education and therapy term "resistance" as used in CPE refers to patterns of relating and communicating that impede the congruence and authenticity of the learning process, individual, or group. These behaviors are mostly unconscious until recognized due to comment by another person, supervisor, or peer. It is sometimes misunderstood as intentional obstruction of the learning program and its goals.

however, he did not arrive at the venue and sent a message that he had a cold and could not participate.

Eager to see how the supervisor would respond, the group used nervously humorous comments to recognize and assert that the group evaluations would need to proceed, and that Van would need to conduct his own self-evaluation with the group in the first session next week. The cohesion among them demanded it.

Expectations of assertive initiative

There emerges in CPE culture an unspoken expectation that a group member will take care of himself interpersonally in group sessions. They will not lapse into long silent withdrawal and quietly refuse to respond to group topics, issues, and projects. They are not allowed to consciously or unconsciously maneuver the group to let them sink into dependence and emotional irresponsibility to shield themselves from confrontation. Habits of interactional dependence eventually stand out in that culture as it is difficult to hide in a small group. In fact, CPE programs in general stand against self-pity, dependence, and habits of unaddressed victimization. One way in which those patterns often become visible is in the reluctance of supervisors to call on quiet members to speak when they don't participate on their own. Other group members can become uncomfortable with the supervisor not prodding a quiet student to participate. The supervisor is more likely to take the attitude that, "Zeke will talk when he has something to say." Other supervisors may use provocative statements like, "Next meeting we'll need to keep Alex quieter." Protecting quiet members and enabling dependent behavior are more likely to be ignored or even suppressed than responded to by repeated invitations for a quiet member to participate.

Confronting (assertive excellence)

Addicts seeking recovery eventually go on to their deaths without a group of people who know how to confront, with astute observation, stark words, immediacy, non-judgmental attitudes, and genuine care for the wellbeing of both themselves and other people. Similarly, CPE group members go on with their fantasies of how well they are doing in mediocre caregiving, unless they find themselves in a group of people who confront them about the patterns that keep their relationships superficially chatty, confusingly incongruent, and grandiosely over-instructional.

In CPE, confrontation means drawing someone's attention to incongruences among their observed behavior, their apparent affect, and their spoken cognition. In other words, it is mentioning directly how what they do in a situation boldly doesn't match what they say they think, or seem to feel. Any given confrontation often points out possible hidden assumptions, unconscious attitudes, and the ignoring or neglect of one's spoken values. A culture rich in confrontations challenges group members to improve their authenticity and the congruence of what they say, what they do, and how they feel. Advancing in the intricate art of confronting one another enlivens a group, keeps members alert for learning in the moment, and rapidly improves self-awareness. Groups that emphasize pervasive hospitality and perpetual congeniality remain quite comfortable but also miss some of the best of what we have for one another.

Immediate conceptualizing

Well into the Group of Six summer of CPE, Sal passionately, sensitively, and descriptively shared with the group the intricate details of how his first two patient death experiences had affected him, as they still lingered in his mind the following day. After hearing the group further draw out his extensive and somewhat pressured intimate sharing, the supervisor quietly suggested that he was referring to the experience of awe. The group took away a memorable learning of what awe is, a potential to name it for themselves in their own future experiences, and a new reverence for awe as a relatively rare and profound experience that is both mystically sacred and utterly human.

A great strength of CPE is its culture of abundant opportunities to apply a concept to a caregiving dynamic immediately, even as the issue is being presented, discussed, and processed in a group context. That allows a rare chance for group members to connect a dynamic or issue with a concept that was once created to efficiently refer to that very issue. The recognition and understanding of "grieving" for example, or "alcoholism," or "PTSD," or "dependent personality," or a thousand other concepts that have only been known socially or academically, can be radically deepened in group members at that moment. Didactic group sessions add considerably to the gradual development of frameworks of understanding people and their troubles in the minds and practices of group members. But no experience compares with immediate conceptualizing in helping them seal that concept into useful understanding, assessment, and practical helping.

Interdisciplinary teams converse with scores of acronyms and concepts as a part of their regular day-to-day conversation and then sometimes even assume those concepts without saying them. The ability to flow with conceptual language as brief references to complex phenomena eases a spiritual caregiver into moving from one hospital unit to another as an effective member[7] of more than one IDT. Writing chart notes with a human-to-human style contributes to that flow as well.

---

7   *Cf.* Hilsman, G.J. (2017) 'Why Record the Intangible in Health Care Culture?' In *Spiritual Care in Common Terms: How Chaplains Can Effectively Describe the Spiritual Needs of Patients in Medical Records.* London: Jessica Kingsley Publishers.

Immediate theologizing[8]

The CPE opportunities for immediate conceptualizing include the highly appropriate cluster of those concepts and terminologies related to theology. Scheduled theological reflection sessions differ considerably from the immediate application of theological concepts to caregiving situations.

As Van in the Group of Six spoke about his goal of becoming more comfortable with the process of people's actual dying, several of the group could recognize that much of the world's religious thinking had been fashioned over centuries to deal with that very moment of a person dying and the depth of emotions, fantasies, and pondering that surround it. CPE lends itself to inviting theological reflection on events and moments as they arise in the group situation from experiences of dying people and others whose wellbeing is seriously threatened.

Theological reflection in a practical sense is bringing new thinking and imagination to situations and relationships that directly consider transcendence or the personal Divine as a part of the data. A chaplain might be beneficially asking themselves, "What would God be saying about this?", "How does this relate to my own way of thinking about ultimate values and questions?", and "What pieces of Scripture, religious history, and the writing of contemporary theologians' apply to this situation and offer some insight into it?" They might even ask, "What bits of popular culture usefully refer to this issue?", such as poetry, song, theater, film, politics and blog. As practical theology, CPE tends to expand and enrich one's theology, and challenge it as well.

---

8 This word is used intentionally in cognizance that is it a mostly Christian term, since there seems to be no currently appropriate word for exploring human issues, relationships, or events, while including traditional and contemporary perceptions of transcendence and faith group efforts to understand and cope with them.

Genuine goal pursuit

A culture in which all group members have communally agreed to pursue genuine goals and to help one another attain them, brings that group together as colleagues, partners, and fellow adventurers into new interpersonal and personal territory. ACPE programs almost invariably begin a process of setting and refining group members' goals in the first week of the program. The clinical method of learning spiritual care is fundamentally goal oriented. As a form of adult education, it functions as if people learn mostly what they want to learn. The goal-setting process is aimed at drawing out what group members are aware of wanting to learn in relation to the program methodologies, the ACPE standards, and the unique caring setting in which the program is functioning.

As the new group member is reflecting on what they want their initial goals to be, they are encouraged to distinguish between authentic goals on the one hand, and a cluster of hopes, dreams, wishes, and high-sounding aspirations that waft about in their mind on the other. They may be asked to reflect on how they want to be different after the program is finished, as a person, a caregiver, a colleague, and/or a professional. They may be urged to think about how progress on their goals will be observable for accountability to other group members, and some of the ways in which they envision beginning pursuit of their goals. They also may be invited to wonder how the group can be involved in their goal pursuit. At the end of the program they may be asked how the goal setting and pursuit had gone for them and what they believe would be new goals prescriptive of the weaknesses in their caregiving practice for possible further CPE or other experiential education programs. In the process, they are becoming more adept at using intentional goals in their continuing education.

Conclusion

ACPE culture can be lost in many ways, but it remains quite resilient when the central methods of its structure are engaged with some expertise. A program flies best when it includes at least one group member who is reaching for the CPE milestones by becoming a process leader, the subject of Part III.

3

Become a Process Leader

Pursue the Milestones in CPE
Professional Development

Becoming a process leader in an ACPE program cannot be hurried and not many CPE participants become interested in doing so. But some do. They change differently from their peers. The changes may not be noticed at first by the group and even by the supervisor. The changes can be elusive, but the history of the ACPE has shown that some of those changes can be observed, validated, and confirmed in ways that bring a maturity as a spiritual clinician to the practice of some group members. Those with the constitution, the astuteness, and the passion for the values and processes of the clinical learning process do more than benefit from CPE. They flourish with it. Aspects of what budding spiritual clinicians look like as described in this part may help the beginning group member to aim for these elements of growth as goals.

In small groups one sees differing ways that people lead. Some become information leaders because of what they know from their previous education, reading, and experience. There are resistance leaders whose subtle or even blatant opposition to the intended growth process can preoccupy other members and reduce their learning. There are compliance leaders whose focus over-concentrates on completing all the required projects well and early, but not necessarily well and authentically. And there are interpersonal authority leaders, the natural power of whose personalities and extroverted initiative carry more influence in group decisions than other members.

Some ACPE program group members, however, eventually become *process leaders*. They come rather quickly to enjoy and excel at facilitating their own progress and the learning of their peers. A few of these, naturally gifted for and fascinated by the human interpersonal dialogue, may become the spiritual clinicians and certified clinical educators of the future.

Like plants in a garden, leadership grows at various rates in ACPE groups. There comes a time when some group members ripen to recognize that they "get" what is happening in the group and glimpse hints of clarity about what is happening within themselves. They then want to take a firmer hold on their own learning process. This remarkable insight often comes in a flash as an eruption of something that has been boiling beneath. In a single group event, or a reflective moment outside it, the realization simply occurs to a group member that they are tuning in to what is "trying to happen" in the group and that they can assist it intentionally. When that budding leader feels the change inside themselves validated by at least one valued authority, they begin to intentionally confirm and nurture it as a transforming cluster of experiences.

Group members that are thus encouraged to continue leading no longer simply comply, just invest in the program as directed, nor even merely succeed. They are attending to the entire process of a CPE group and seeking ways to enrich it, to further nurture it, to help it along and facilitate individual peer relationships in their group. Typically, they have noticed a bit of what the supervisor does and joined her. At that point, they have reached a certain maturity as group members and will benefit accordingly. Others have simply found their own gifted uniqueness that fits clinical spiritual care and will run with it, regardless of the supervisor's preferences.

Organizational attempts in the ACPE have long recognized this advancing group member milestone. Supervisors have sought to describe specific indicators that this change has happened to a given group member. "Advanced standing" was used for acknowledging this progress pacer in the 1970s and 1980s. Two mostly unspoken primary indicators of readiness for that designation at the time were: 1) an ability to assertively stay connected with the group even when being challenged; and 2) the ability to make active, less defensive, practical *use of feedback* offered by the group and supervisor, changing their behavior relatively quickly, experimenting to improve their personal identity and their spiritual care.

In the 1990s the language changed. A new distinction between Level I and Level II CPE, subsequently in the ACPE Standards, was based on this marked advancing change in process leading students. The essential defining criteria distinguishing the two levels was initially that Level I outcomes were, in general, focused on more basic, personal, internal issues, while those of Level II were directed towards external, professional relationships and competencies. The widespread assumption was that Level I outcome issues would likely be a part of the personal makeup of an intern or resident all her life as a professional caregiver, but that they had been identified and addressed enough to, for the most part, keep them from detracting from the quality of their caregiving and colleague relationships.

In Chapter 6 we will interpret the official objectives and outcomes of the current (2017) ACPE Standards. What follows here is an effort to further refine the partially observable indicators of this waypoint of professional development, emphasizing the group member's improved capacities to function as a process leader and, eventually, professional caregiver. There are eight.

Initiative and persistence in group process

This growth shows itself in consistency of offering both validation and critique in the group. An observer would see the advancing group member offering significant feedback on every presentation of their peers and injecting cogent input on nearly every group dynamics issue. They seem to be emerging in the group life as taking on a responsibility for their active, consistent participation that can be relied on to enrich the group process. They take initiative to validate what they like in a peer's verbatim report for example, and ask pertinent, crisply worded questions about what they don't. Even if they are the only group member reaching this milestone at this particular time, they can be counted on to help keep the group feedback flowing, for the most part avoiding giving subtly disingenuous flattery on the one hand and hurtful, vaguely hostile criticism on the other.

Subtle negative sentiment, a kind of professional jealousy, can sometimes be detected brewing inside the peers of that advancing person.

Conflict in the group provides another window into the emergence of process leading peers. Learning to deal effectively with conflict, including making quick decisions about which indications of emerging conflict to ignore, constitutes a significant maturing in preparation for a career of professional caregiving.

The advancing group member becomes gradually aware of how they habitually relate internally to this latent conflict and what they tend to do when it erupts into overt verbal and emotional skirmishes. As conflicting interactions occur in the group, they learn and change. They take on different, new behaviors that supplant their old patterns such as avoidance, heightened anxiety, excessive appeasing, impulsive verbal-snapping aggression, and reflexive interpersonal peacemaking. They devise direct questions bolstered by group practice confidence, and are seen functioning with persistence beyond merely raising issues. They show plucky courage in staying with the conflicted air that seems to fill the room.

This conflict solidity serves them well in delivering patient care. Professional helping contexts such as healthcare culture teem with staff member conflicts both overt and chronically underlying, in the service of keeping the essential medical and nursing work primary. Gaining a bit of confidence in deciding when, where, and especially whether to initiate conversation about personal and relational issues constitutes progress in becoming a professional caregiver of any discipline, capable of occasionally deciding to raise latent conflicts to the surface and helping to open them for facilitation and, possibly, temporary resolution.

Ease of theological reflection

A 2004 journal article reported on a study of 80 applicants for Association of Professional Chaplains (APC) certification who had failed the interview attempt.[1] The purpose of the study was to determine what standards of competence were most often lacking in applicants for certification. In the study results, two standards emerged as the most difficult for applicants at the time. One of them was the relative inability to bring a theological perspective to spiritual caregiving situations during the interview.[2] It appears that academic theology and clinical education for ministry had failed to stimulate their ability to be practical with their theology. Despite a master's degree in divinity, which is the most common academic grounding for ordination, and a year of clinical challenge of their caregiving cases, many of them had failed in the basic capacity to see their caregiving as theological in the real situations of ministry.

CPE programs have had their times of leaning more towards psychology than theology, skewing the blend of the two widely

---

1   Grossoehme, D.H. (2004) 'Patterns of unmet competencies by first time candidates for APC Board Certification.' *Chaplaincy Today 20*, 2, Fall/Winter, 13–16.

2   The other was medical ethics knowledge and competence.

towards the former. Ease of fluidity in finding congruent theological perspectives on one's caregiving work became thin. In one of the best-known books of the clinical ministry field psychologist Paul Pruyser challenged chaplains and pastoral educators to look more closely at how they had abandoned the established and even classical concepts of theology, developed over centuries to help people spiritually, in favor of the modern frameworks of practical and even pop psychology.[3] That direct critique, almost scolding in tone, prompted clinical ministry educators to shift back on the continuum to begin using the rather new educational methodology called *theological reflection*. They began to regain the old language and integrate it into ACPE group members' caregiving, to increase their ability to talk about theological perspectives with confidence as practical theology, using both descriptive and theological terms.

On the other hand, many members of ACPE groups enter clinical education programs immersed in theological perspectives, almost devoid of experience in efforts to actually help people who are severely challenged spiritually with what is happening to them physically and interpersonally. Some of these bring extensive study of the Hebrew and Christian scriptures or the Koran or Buddhist traditions, and strong convictions about their teachings for which they would fight and even die as martyrs. But when they face real people caught in real personal and physical dilemmas, they can quite quickly find such dogma quite useless in favor of what seems to work in actual care of people. The path of integration of theology and the behavioral sciences generally needs facilitation by a supervisor and peers who can ask pointed and prescriptive questions of one another in the midst of a single group effort to understand just what a given patient actually seems to need.

Some indicators that applicants for certification have gained this integrative capacity include seeing them rather easily and smoothly speak about a case being discussed, applying values and concepts

---

3   Pruyser, P. (1976) *The Minister as Diagnostician: Personal Problems in Pastoral Perspective*. Louisville, KY: Westminster John Knox Press.

from sacred writings and issues from the history of the major faith groups, and references to what recent theologians have published about the issues in the case. There is a smoothness of flow in the theologizing, quickness of imagination, a creative application of metaphor, a breadth of considering what to include from scripture and other resources, and a perception that there is a solidity in the group member's grounding in a philosophical level position that fits their personality and religious history.

Consultative expertise

As a group member grows through additional units of CPE, the focus generally shifts a little from processing verbatim sessions to *case study presentation* that may include segments of verbatim material from several visits with the same patient and family. This broader communal consideration of spiritual care situations further expands all of the group members' ability to care extensively as well as intensively for hospitalized people and those in other life-pinching situations. One of the skills that furthers this educational advancement is knowing when and how to consult colleagues and other professionals about one's work.

If there is one cluster of abilities that defines the hoped-for results of ACPE program engagement it is this ability to confidently and courageously seek consultation, defined here as *making yourself vulnerable to the perspectives of trusted others regarding specifics of your spiritual care work efforts.* Etymologically, consulting means "striking together," and in CPE it refers to a cluster of abilities in collaborating with one another about actual cases those involved.

Organizational managers and administrators hire consultants because to some degree they believe they have exhausted the creativity and resources they already have, and need a fresh look at the way they do their work, configure their policies and procedures, and make practical use of the hired experts already available to them. They agree to listen to and consider seriously what outside experts with positive reputations tell them about what they see, consider their assessments, and think carefully about their recommendations.

Similarly, when spiritual caregivers encounter gnarly patient or family situations, they do well to meet the needs the best they can at the time and then consider consulting about the case. Most often this begins with simply asking a colleague that one trusts at least to a degree, to listen and then both validate and critique. The ACPE verbatim session is essentially shaped to help people over time to develop that cluster of skills called consulting.

In the group member who is honing the capacity to consult well, the supervisor notices several things, sometimes even before the student does. They see that person remembering in-the-moment, key past interpersonal events of their history that relate to this caregiving event and that unconsciously shaped it, impeding its effectiveness. They watch that verbalized remembering as it contributes additional insight to the group processing. They see an ease of hearing and considering the pointed, cogent but often unpalatable suggestions and observations that come from their peers. They hear acknowledgement of "aha" moments of realizing some elements of their caregiving patterns that influence their care of entire classes of patients. And at times they hear mention of concepts from that person's reading and study that are spontaneously applied to the dynamics occurring in group dialogue in the moment.

The benefits of consulting well are considerable. Many group members go away from CPE programs having almost completely misunderstood their purpose and their value. As it is with marriage and parenting, only experience teaches how to consult well while letting go of regrets about what might have, or should have, gone better. The communal learning from group sessions also takes a quantum leap forward as the highly successful group member moves towards another level of maturing in the caregiving profession. The entire group generally matures a bit too. And those who master this milestone carry the skills and attitudes of consulting well with them ever after.

Self-supervision

As successful ACPE group members engage the learning process elements, they are, in a real sense, taking the group and supervisor into their minds and hearts, carrying them there forever. The integration that results from vigorous use of the clinical method of learning incorporates into group members' lasting memory and habitual practice the best of the critique and validation of one's CPE peers and supervisors. We faintly hear the group's voices and see the supervisor's facial impression in the back of our minds while figuring out what is the best move forward during tough and complex patient cases as they arise in our careers. The ability to access that trove of CPE experiences for insight and attitude in present cases is called self-supervision.

This ability may look like over-self-reliance from the outside, but it is the opposite. Having one's mentors and peers with you—inside you in a sense—in patient care, increases confidence and professional maturity. It is parallel to the growing ability of an adult to increasingly take care of their own physical health, until at a certain point recognizing the clear need to access professional care before the physical damages and disease processes progress beyond repair.

What a certified educator is liable to see that signals that a group member's self-supervision is flourishing is heard in the stories they tell about their caregiving cases. These are characterized by richness of data about a given case, various perspectives on the data, creativity in what was tried in the care provided, perspicacious use of conceptual language to represent the assessment and care, noting of the complex feelings of the various people involved in the case (including their own), and a reasonable disposition, resolution, or conclusion to the case situation.

Near-universal human-to-human caregiving rapport

As ACPE group members are initially charged with the care of all people in a specific unit of care, they begin to be challenged to relate helpfully to some people who are far different from themselves. They are responsible for listening carefully to homeless, addicted, mentally ill people, highly dependent individuals, and other personality disordered folks, as well as those of privilege and those of ethnic cultures completely foreign to that caregiver's language and entire life experience. Not all of these, of course, are ready and waiting to talk personally. They need the creation of a listening context that differs radically from what most of them find in day-to-day life.

Tendencies of neophyte caregivers to favor, consciously or unconsciously, patients of their own religious background, geographical history, or ethnic culture shrink the range of people they can help. The challenge to broaden that range calls forth the natural impetus to develop new abilities and skills needed to establish rapport on a pragmatic, human-to-human level. Those group members who excel at this broadening of attitude and skill bring far more useful perspectives to the group processing of all issues, including spiritual care of their own peer group members at crucial times of need. They are showing the new maturity of those who have grown to invest broadly in the CPE learning process and the field of clinical spiritual care.

The caregiving skills that make up this new breadth of care include basic ones from initial CPE, such as initiating patient conversation, establishing rapport, and deepening the interaction beyond socializing—basic skills that naturally invite personal disclosure by most any human. They also include, however, complicated ways of deepening conversations from initial rapport—making appraisals of personal resources and needs of people in difficult life situations; ending conversations at key moments that fit the relationship's unfolding; artful referral that is a bit difficult for patients to resist; and reporting orally and in writing on the patient care one provides, to interdisciplinary staff and other spiritual caregivers in ways that are helpful and not merely compliant or subtly self-referencing. In short, these new abilities honed to a satisfying level of expertise constitute a near-universal ability to establish caregiving rapport with most anyone in any kind of physical or interpersonal need. This approaches a professional level of competence ready for certification and employment. And it brings a new level of expertise to their CPE groups.

Growing colleagueship

An observable level of growing confidence in colleagueship emerges in maturing group members as they increase collaborative working and socializing with peer group members, staff chaplains, treatment staff clinicians, and even mentoring supervisors. Once considered to be the defining characteristic of some certification processes, genuine confident colleagueship remains a key observable indicator of a new level of studenthood and service in budding chaplains. They seem to "get" the roles of physicians and nurses in a more sophisticated way, honoring those very different disciplines' central contributions to care and wanting to help them with their unique roles and values, as colleagues not adversaries that they think "should honor chaplains" more, and make a place for them at the table of staff deliberations. Caregivers of other disciplines with whom progressing CPE group members work are heard to comment on the good work of those ascending students. They speak of them as colleagues rather than as mere students that they are required to help and easily excuse for barely adequate care. Confident joining of interdisciplinary teams towards the satisfaction of enduring professional belonging will be a sure sign of an advancing ACPE group member. As Earl Nightingale once quipped, "excellence always sells."

New levels of colleagueship are noticed by supervisors and others in the way a group member speaks with a level of authority between the slightly strident image management of a "poser" and the palpable reticent aloofness of a neophyte. The student with this new level of teaming stands behind their perceptions of patients and peers in ways that are difficult to deflect or ignore. In consulting with IDT staff members, they are convincing to them about the spiritual needs of people who are patients. This surprising level of personal and professional authority can bring a smile to observing experienced clinicians, and it can annoy CPE peers who have been passed upon the learning curve of developing professional functioning. Inspiring confidence in those around them, these new individuals are emerging from their role as fledgling novices. That observation delights those who are genuinely interested in their development.

Colleagueship also includes the observable capacity of providing care for CPE group peers when they need it despite conflict with one or more (or all) of them. An old CPE adage holds that a student accustomed to caring for patients and learning from peers has become advanced or ready for Level II when they can learn from their patients and care for their peers. Collegial empathy that can be counted on at inconvenient and even awkward times remains an assessment indicator of budding maturity today.

Professional goal investment

Some theology students tire of setting academic and personal growth goals, incessantly being asked to please professors and formation officials who they see as needing from them only compliance, unable to view students from the whole person perspective of actual human beings. Facing a group of ACPE program peers as diverse budding caregivers who are consistently asking them good questions changes that. That rugged experience rather vigorously prods them to think of themselves critically and talk about themselves straightforwardly, in genuine work to find what they want to learn, how they want to change, and how they want to be different at the end of that particular three-month program. They are learning a new process that distinguishes authentic goals from vague dreams, earnest hopes, and high-sounding aspirations. It focuses on what that group member needs when in touch with their genuine weaknesses as a caregiver, as a clinical student, and as a person.

Those group members who meet the challenge of defining goals based on self-understanding and serious consideration of their professional weaknesses as targets for continuing professional competence move ahead in professional development. They can be seen challenging the goal-setting process of others, and experiencing a maturity of taking charge of their own learning process. Common initial goals of "I want to be a better listener," or "I want to improve my self-care," or "I want to learn about hospital ministry" contain little enough specificity to be mostly useless in clinical education. Advancing group members are more likely to challenge the generalities of goal setting in their peers towards prodding development of greater specificity, prescriptive focus on weaknesses, and accountability to group peers. The little truth contained in generalizations produces nothing memorable or transformative. With an intense context of interpersonal challenge, the process of setting goals for oneself begins to deepen immediately and eventually can become a lifelong process of keeping one eye always on one's own lacuna in the quiver of their caregiving skill, even in those who eventually become true experts in their caregiving fields.

A physician friend of mine has remarked with bold dismay several times to me that most of his colleagues, "don't read!" It is easy for professionals of all disciplines to lapse into passive reliance on what they already know and how they can already function. The solid but not strident commitment to continual development as a caregiver emerges for a repetitive process of looking at one's weaknesses, defining goals that address those weaknesses, and then facing a group challenge of how others see those goals as having a chance of improving on them. Those who can make themselves vulnerable several times by presenting in writing their very best efforts at finding fitting goals that meet immediate needs in their caregiving competence not only learn more, but they incorporate a goal-setting process into their personality that lives long after formative education ceases.

Astute evaluative description

Excellent written description combines at least two very different skills. Writing clearly on the one hand comes together with evaluating without moralistic negative judgment on the other. They gradually come together in CPE whenever a group member is asked to submit written evaluative comments on a peer in a rich group process setting. The project of group evaluative experiences is to simply and clearly describe one's peers in writing that will be read in the assembled presence of those peers, and then processed with how they see both the evaluator and the one being evaluated. Strengths and weaknesses as a caregiver form a key part of the evaluation criteria. Another is the ease with which the evaluating peer consults with the other group members. The advancing group member seems to do this with an accuracy that is easily validated by the peers.

When you enter and engage in this process with courage, sensitivity, careful wording, and evaluative comments that your other peers can seriously consider, and do so with some level of consistency, then you have reached a waypoint of formation as a valuable colleague caregiver. Your narrative entries into the medical record are likely improving as well.

Conclusion

These eight descriptions of advancing ACPE group members are never as ideal as they may sound above. The group clinical learning process remains earthily human, with only unpredictably surprising indicators of a given group member's growing process leadership. That huge human factor phenomenon leads us to acknowledging the limitations of this fine educational process called CPE.

4

Befriend Your Own Spiritual Development

A Phenomenological Theory for CPE

The beginning CPE student may initially assume that this program focuses on learning about the people being served in the facility in which the program is set and how to help them better. It is of course. But they soon find out, often as early as the application interview, that it is equally aimed at them. The attitude they develop about that determines to a great degree how successful they will be in the program. They will do best to befriend their own human and spiritual development, and grow some courageous curiosity about how they have been the principal shaper of the ways their human agency serves their evolving human spirit.

It is reasonable to assume that a primary reason that nurses and physicians have not gone far in including spiritual assessment in their work is that they have not ventured into exploring and clarifying the spiritual and religious development theme in their own life history. That self-exploration is not necessary in their fields of helping people. Spiritual caregivers, however, cannot maintain that same persistent vague awareness of the way they have been shaped by their history of meeting the uncontrollable world. A year or two of engagement in ACPE programs constitutes the most integrative process by which professional chaplains and other spiritual caregivers prepare for entering the highly complex and ultimately mysterious aspect of patients' lives called their unique spiritualities.

As various spiritual care conversations are processed in the CPE group and in individual supervision, it becomes clear that caregiving interactions are intersubjective, radically engaging, and interdepending on the parties involved. Under clinical exploration of a single caregiving conversation it is easily seen that the caregiver's own inner workings have heavily influenced the content and character of the care as it unfolded. That caregiver is then faced with the project of understanding their own personal history as it affects their current relationships. Since not all that personal discovery may be seen by them as positive, they will need courage and calm curiosity to continue pursuing their clinical education. They will best befriend the bold elements of their own spiritual development reasonably accurately as it can be remembered, rather than cling to the assumption that it has all been just fine, or horribly dysfunctional.

Indeed, it has been all very acceptable. It has been functional, either adequately or minimally supportive of the various aspects of their life. It wasn't until they decided to engage in education for the depth and professionally intimate endeavor of chaplaincy care that it emerges as patchily inadequate, and then not terminally so. Finding that the development of their human spirit has not well prepared them for this field of work is normal, almost universal. Just because their spiritual development has not been optimal doesn't mean they are somehow hopelessly damaged. They may choose to enter a form of therapy to better understand themselves and some of the life events that have thrown them. But in doing so they will be healing previous personal woundedness, expanding the usefulness of their own person in preparation for the care of others. What Brene Brown wrote recently, "If we can share our story with someone who responds with empathy and understanding, shame can't survive"[1] applies to chaplaincy as well as psychotherapy, Catholic confession when conducted well, and AA sponsor relationships.

The elements of spiritual development

How we humans meet the uncontrollable world weaves its way as a primary theme running through our histories. At the very beginning of our encountering the world, as infants and toddlers, we wordlessly incorporate the reality that we can influence our surroundings. After that we are constantly sorting out what we can do from what we can get others to do, and from what we simply cannot do. The word *influence* refers to a "flowing into, "[2] or literally a moving of one fluid combining itself with another liquid, changing both. Our reverie is basically a flow of our influences. Our conversations constitute a flow of stories about what has significantly influenced us, got our attention, and somehow changed us. Even if we were "spoiled" as toddlers, we knew from our direct experience that we can't always get our way—but sometimes we can. Those events in which we do get our desires happen in ways that are incessantly elusive to capture. Sometimes it seems like our words command our parenting one's actions, and sometimes not. We can run faster than Billy but not Johnny.

Then there are those events in which we know we have no influence at all. Old Spot dies, Grandpa won't play, and Daddy can't stop the rain. Even when they pray as fervently as their hearts will allow, some children cannot stop their night incontinence, remove the complexities imposed on them by childhood diabetes, or get as much attention as their cuter sister. If we're fortunate, it eventually occurs to us that everything of importance is a *confluence*, a "flowing together" of two or many powers, making it frustratingly impossible

---

1   Brown, B. (2015) *Daring Greatly: How the Courage to Be Vulnerable Transforms the Way We Live, Love, Parent, and Lead.* New York: Avery Penguin, p.74.
2   From the Latin, "in" combined with *fluere*, to flow.

to comprehend or control, but sometimes rich, hopeful, and exciting to try.

Whatever we do, think, or come to believe about that stark reality of life grows into what can pragmatically be called our spiritual life.

Specific experiences catalyze the shaping of this unique spirituality that is our own. There is not yet a cohesive, written conceptualization of how human spirituality develops, despite the substantial efforts of fine minds to portray it in developmental psychology,[3] religious tradition,[4] and spiritual care research writing.[5] The building blocks of our spiritualities seem to be episodic, almost random events that boldly either built on or impeded the flourishing of our happiness. Only a few dramatic childhood events stick in our memories, seemingly without reason. Why we remember these and not those other father events, sibling conflicts, teacher eyes, or church class instructions, eludes us.

From this perspective, we are all unique storytellers of how people, groups, and communities have influenced us. We relate with one another largely through telling the stories of what has affected us. Funny stories raise our happiness by seeing and hearing the delight of others when we share them. Sad stories gain us some empathy with the misfortune of others, or a bit of support for our sadness (or indeed some pity from our delicious victimization). The intensity of our angry stories drains some of the displeasure from the offenses and injustices we feel (or escalates the energizing excitement of being unjustly treated). The stories of what we regret cut our guilt in half as we share or "confess" them (or burgeons into deadening but familiar remorse). Stories of our embarrassing moments take some of the sting out of having felt belittled. All day long we tell our stories or

---

3   Fowler, J. (1995) *Stages of Faith: The Psychology of Human Development and the Quest for Meaning.* San Francisco, CA: Harper One.

4   Rohr, R. (2011) *Falling Upward: A Spirituality for the Two Halves of Life.* San Francisco, CA: Jossey Bass Publishers.

5   Roehlkepartain, E.C., Ebstyne King, E., Wagener, L.M. and Benson, P.L. (2005) *The Handbook of Spiritual Development in Childhood and Adolescence.* Los Angeles, CA: Sage Publications.

quietly form them to be told later. Lovers and friends rejoice in having found a listener to the little, and occasionally big, stories of our days. "How was your day?" classically opens up this flow that, in one way or another, feeds our human spirit whenever we can find the context that promotes it.

Much of what we are naturally compelled to share comes out in stories that are not altogether happy. These are the nudging concerns, un-worded fears, unintended slights, thoughtless insults, and shading disappointments that quietly grey our mood. Other stories fly a bit lower in such eventualities as potential surgeries, job losses, lover squabbles, and friend misunderstandings that drag on us a bit harder. And then there are the more life-injuring events that instead of being shared, become intentional secrets and unintentional inabilities to recount them to anyone—events, fears, and hurts that have so dismayed us that we never tell them. Combat stories, rape stories, domestic abuse stories, neglect in childhood stories, bullying stories—all tend to lie dormant, along with the deep hurts, terrifying fears, and burdening feelings of regret that accompany them. Love breakups and broken friendships are relational events in which the untellable stories mount up until they so damage the flow of stories that the relationships become irreparable. Estrangement and breakups are essentially blocked relationships that stop the sharing of any stories at all.

Chaplaincy is a field that elicits stories from people that they cannot, or have not yet been able to, tell or relate sufficiently for them to heal. It is the intricate creating of an interpersonal context in which the stories move increasingly to the surface of a person's consciousness, and then begin to pop out beyond any intention. Becoming a chaplain or a skilled spiritual caregiver is learning the art of informally helping people overcome the barriers to their telling of as-yet untold or untellable stories of all kinds.[6] ACPE group members often comment on how the content of verbatim presentations are

---

6   Jerome Bruner (2003) *Making Stories: Law, Literature and Life*, p.93. Boston: Harvard University Press.

not precisely verbatim, that the presenter's memory is easily altered by what they would like to have said, and their ego invested in them looking a bit better than the actual verbatim conversation would reveal. But that mixing of imagination and memory doesn't seem to deter the benefits that come from encountering the presenter and eliciting their associations in the moment about the patient and their own complex inner processes. Psychologist Jerome Bruner describes the way imagination and memory combine inextricably in the telling, "Through narrative, we construct, reconstruct, in some ways reinvent yesterday and tomorrow. Memory and imagination fuse in the process....Memory and imagination supply and consume each other's wares."

From that point of view, CPE is the preparing of persons for that art of interpersonal care of people's untold or inadequately told stories.

Phenomenology in CPE

Far more of our soul-shaping events are available to us than we normally recall. Some of the troubling ones are inextricably tied together in what Freud called neurosis and Jung called complexes. Those impeding stories can become operationalized by current, emotionally charged events that pull them out of us and influence our behavior just below our awareness. We can then recall them into consciousness, especially with interpersonal assistance. To the point of this book, these unconscious, life-shaping memories of a caregiver sometimes emerge in the context of the rich intimate conversations spiritual caregivers have with patients who are in real-life predicaments. With close examination, sometimes they can be processed during a verbatim presentation or the oral recounting of a jolting group interchange that evokes emotions like those enkindled by the original event that occurred even decades before.

The CPE experience commonly invites group members to talk about past experiences that are found to have created memories that unconsciously—and then partially consciously—have been seen in verbatim conversations to affect their spiritual care conversations. An implicit assumption in that practice includes that some memories affect us more deeply than others and shape us as we mature. Based on that assumption, it may be possible to theorize that such highly influential memories fall into loose categories. Put together in a logical way these become a framework of spiritual development that is useful in bringing cognitive perspective to a spiritual life's development and to the entire endeavor of CPE explorations. The following constitutes a phenomenological framework for looking at one's own spiritual development in very practical terms.

Edmund Husserl was a turn-of-the-twentieth-century philosopher who originated a branch of that field called phenomenology.[7] The core of that thinking was advanced by the existentialist therapies that resulted from his ideas, which influenced the creation of CPE. The early CPE practitioners picked up on Husserl's observation that a person never knows the essential core, the true reality (the *noumena*) of things and other people. He called what we do perceive, the *phenomenon*, the thing or person as it *appears* to us. Existentialists then emphasized the process of *accurate description* as the best we can do to apprehend someone and share our observations with them and among us.

That notion had a strong effect on the field of clinical chaplaincy. As the clinical ministry field developed in the 1920s, chaplains began to pick up on aspects they noticed about people, described them in conveyed empathy, and then saw that person continue to disclose more than she even intended to say. Today's chaplains variously use the same approach. Much of what a patient says has apparently been unconscious, unknown to the person themselves, until they begin to articulate it and hear it responded to by another person. Then it can sometimes flow out vividly into their mind and words simultaneously (and sometimes not). This phenomenon itself was extremely useful in both chaplaincy and clinical education.

---

7   Husserl, E. (1913/1967) *Ideas: General Introduction to Phenomenology*. New York: Collier Books.

For discussion, to make the complexity of that mass of life-shaping events manageable for theorizing, we can assume that three clusters of such shaping memories unfold as we develop physically, mentally, socially, and emotionally, the sum of which is our own unique spirituality. We could name the three components: *heritage*, or what developed in us consciously and unconsciously through relationships and responses to vivid experiences in childhood; *thinking*, or what has arisen by the various uses of our minds as they develop, and the intersubjective relationships in which we share them; and life-shaking *experiences that nearly overwhelmed us*, positively and negatively, with the obviously uncontrollable.

We all carry with us a sparse history of our spiritual coping and enjoying of all that is quite obviously beyond us. First, in our spiritual heritage, we were bequeathed early experiences and concepts by our pristine encounters with the natural world and by those people we watched or who seriously engaged us when we were children. Second, we gradually began to think for ourselves and make decisions based on our own cognition, perceptions, and intuition, forming beliefs and convictions that partially guide our behavior and sometimes conflict with our childhood perceptions and beliefs. And third, we have had shaking adult experiences that have challenged our very core, adding to the perpetually changing uniqueness that is our own spiritual way. All of these have combined in intricate, partially observable ways, making up our functional spirituality, which sustains us, until it can't, in the midst of uncontrollable events such as some of those that require hospitalization.

The value of immediacy

A primary feature of chaplaincy is that of availability. A patient who would never request a chaplain may be suspicious when one arrives in their hospital room and introduces themselves. They may even send the chaplain away with refusal, based on some historically experienced personal mistreatment or on having heard of some religious atrocity by a spiritual leader. But then, because the chaplain is here, now, and appears to be both kind and savvy, they blurt out a few nasty or sad words and the conversation has begun. The chaplain's physical presence, emotional availability, and earthy understanding compelled them to engage, and then receive care they never would have sought for themselves.

Similarly, a CPE intern submits a verbatim report to the group because they are on the schedule and have had conversations with patients they found strangely interesting, subtly threatening, or surprisingly warming. As they talk about that patient conversation with the assembled group, they find themselves entering an emotional state beyond what they expected. Then a peer, after the group has conveyed empathy in some successful way, asks one more pointed question. The intern, in a split second or a few of them, relates the patient to a specific event or person in their history that is still laden with emotion. They recognize the influence that past story has had on their relationship with the patient, and begins being flooded with how it may have influenced several of their relationships and perhaps even established a pattern in their relating ever since. It is difficult to see how that insight and partial healing could have happened outside the context of an astute peer group such as this. Even group therapy may not include as much immediacy of attention to relational functioning, since it doesn't regularly bring current helping relationships of group members into the group interaction.

The new ACPE group member may seek to shield themselves from such shaking events, but in doing so robs themselves of some of the best learning of their life. Telling the underlying stories of their shaping at these precise times sometimes frees them for far more intimate caregiving contact with patients and peers. CPE is not designed to create little therapists, but rather advantageous interlopers that hear and facilitate stories that need to be told for enhancement of the health of the human spirit. CPE brings fluidity to caregivers' familiarity with their own troubling and victorious stories, preparing them to better hear the stories of others. Their own stories tend to be of three kinds: those from their heritage, from their developing cognition, and from the remarkable encounters with the dramatically uncontrollable world.

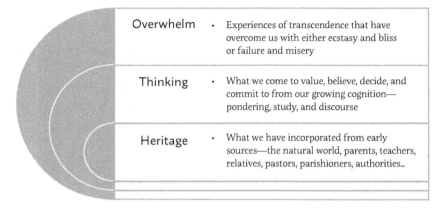

Overwhelm	•	Experiences of transcendence that have overcome us with either ecstasy and bliss or failure and misery
Thinking	•	What we come to value, believe, decide, and commit to from our growing cognition—pondering, study, and discourse
Heritage	•	What we have incorporated from early sources—the natural world, parents, teachers, relatives, pastors, parishioners, authorities...

Figure 4.1 Stages of spiritual development: the capacity to cope with and enjoy the uncontrollable

Heritage—Spiritual DNA?

We are all heirs to how the people around us meet uncontrollable reality, as well as to our own childhood experiences of it. Our spiritual heritage, like our DNA, is our starting point. It sets the stage for decisions we make later. There is no well-defined point of distinction between spiritual heritage and our own reflective influence on our human spirit. They intertwine in inexplicable ways to produce who we are. But roughly what we do with what is beyond us before we begin to take charge of our own lives constitutes our spiritual heritage. Some of the more common elements of this earliest shaping—the source of much of the hindrance of our caregiving relationships—include the following.

MOM

As infants we rely first and heavily on "mothering ones" for supplying what we need in the immediate moment, our only purview at the time. Experiencing the world so soon as the only "Higher Power," the new budding person began to fashion a personality of either deep trusting confidence or near permanent mistrust of the entire Beyond. According to developmental theorist Erik Erikson, too much unsettling unpredictability in those crucial first months outside the womb almost invariably results in significant lifelong psychopathology and major difficulties with belonging ever after.

"Mother" remains an archetype that contains stories of our own mothers and other mothering—ones that evoke warmth, sadness, anger, gratitude, avoidances, deep hurts, and fears of abandonment in all people everywhere. CPE group members' stories about mothers seem to be lying underneath consciousness virtually all the time. Patients who remind us on some level of our mothers compel us to talk about Mom, as patterns of behavior are often seen to be connected to how we related to her as our first Higher Power. Some of that talk will bring tears of nostalgic joy, and occasionally bring forth healing by ameliorating habits that tend to sabotage our relationships.

DAD

Jungian authors Robert Moore and Douglas Gillette[8] promoted the notion that there is in every man, in differing proportions, a king, a warrior, a magician, and a lover. If he has children, all of these affect his children's budding spirituality. A man's internal king administrates, decides for the best of the whole person, and needs to be in charge of his actions most of the time. The warrior emerges when the man or his loved ones are in danger in some way, and ought not to rule the man in peaceful times. The magician can "make it happen," pull things off, get it done, in ways that may seem

---

8   Gillette, D. and Moore, R. (1991) *King, Warrior, Magician, Lover: Rediscovering the Archetypes of the Mature Masculine.* San Francisco, CA: Harper One.

gloriously mysterious to children. And the lover rises to the occasion of relating to a romantic partner, feeding the elusive liveliness of that relationship over time, and negotiating the ever-changing complexities of intimate relationships of deep emotional connection and passionate carnal love.

Like all mysteries of human experience, the influence of a father on the spirituality of offspring cannot be controlled or completely understood. Despite careful efforts to teach and mold, what fathers say pales in comparison to how children see their father act. What makes him laugh, what interests him, how does he relate to them, and especially to their mother? How does he deal with problems? How does he treat and talk about people of cultures, ethnicities, and lifestyles that differ greatly from his? What frustrates him, and what angers him? What are his dreams, and how does he deal with not attaining them? There is no managing this kind of patterned or unconscious interaction, and it will be the source of much transference—exaggerated emotion embedded in some human interactions— in the child's adult years as a CPE group member.

SIBLINGS

Those who lived in the same house and were "little like us" when it seemed like everybody else was big, had their early influence on our spirit. It is said that we develop our first morality in relationship to our siblings and toddler friends, prior to any prepared teaching. There we shape our initial levels of compassion, competition, judgment, fairness, and our first ways of dealing with anger, hurt, sadness, delight, guilt, and shame. These are likely to be the longest relationships we will ever have, and there is no guarantee of them being positive. They affected our development powerfully, as they are likely to continue influencing the spirit of our days ever after— and certainly our caregiving relationships as well.

FRIENDS (BOTH GIRLS AND BOYS)

From the time we are toddlers, we are influenced by the people we like or those we respond to because they seem to like us, and easily find out that we simply cannot completely manage them. Some of the characteristics we possess in which our toddler relationships show delight become etched into our minds as positive traits and treasured physical attributes. Those of our characteristics they seem to want to correct, improve, or deliberately ignore, we may ignore too, or let them feed the tendency to feel bad about ourselves. The rejection of expressed or implied disgust by bullies is probably no more powerful than rejection or perceived insouciance of those peer people we inexplicably admire.

Those boys and girls that stand out as ones we especially like, in the latent budding sexuality of childhood, are far more likely to be remembered in the joy of seeing their glory serendipitously or the sensing the sting of their faces when they are annoyed or disgusted with us. Those events are shaping our later self-concepts of ourselves as lovers, in background sentiments of ourselves as either attractive or dull. As with Charlie Brown and the "little red-haired girl"[9] we may frequently remember one idealized nursery school friend even if we never even had a conversation with her. A unique patient may suddenly remind us of that person, causing us to quickly overcome a longstanding avoidance of caring for patients that are physically and personally more attractive to us than any others.

This theme obviously picks up again, almost overwhelming us, in adolescent romance.

NATURE

In our early years, as we began to touch the realities beyond our immediate relationships, encounters with the natural world coalesced

---

9   Schulz, C. (1950) Syndicated Cartoon. See King, D. Charlie Brown Never Found His Little Red-Haired Girl, but We Did, *Vanity Fair's HWD Newsletter*, November 6, 2015. Accessed on 11/11/2017 at www.vanityfair.com/hollywood/2015/11/peanuts-real-little-red-haired-girl

with what we garnered from our relationships. It was quickly clear that the beauty of the natural world—in animals, the sky, the storm, or an autumn pond for example—was nearly overwhelming and defied words in the days when we had so few. And that world also impinged upon us with examples of the ruthlessness of that same natural environment. It emerged imperceptibly that our place in the continuum of power was simple and unthinkingly accepted. When the electricity would go out in Iowa where I was raised, mom would get us kids huddled around a candle listening to the storm, knowing we were either lucky or blessed to be warm and deliciously excited at the power just outside. Similarly obvious was the inability to catch as many fish as we wanted, beckon forth the squirrel from our plum tree, or keep the pigeons from waking us all too early just outside my bedroom window. If we were lucky enough to have a family pet, the dog, and perhaps especially the cat, showed us we may have influence but never control over their affection. And some neighborhood dogs would bite. The influence of the natural world on our human spirits starts early and lasts a lifetime. It no doubt began at the dawn of humanity itself.

ELDERS

The attitudes of elders about the unpredictable had their influence on our spiritual formation too, on what stances and skills we developed early. Perhaps it was our intuitive knowing that they had lived longer or their kind and knowing eyes on us, or their quirky humor that seemed hatched to make us laugh. How they regarded us, ignored us, turned towards others, carried us, or abused us at unpredictable times, stayed in our minds as part of the DNA that contributes to guiding us. Venturing very far into nature requires some knowledge, some experience, and some lore, that we first got from those who were older and cared. Who was it whose savvy helped us dare to hike and camp in that alien world? How did teachers regard us, and what place did we take in their classrooms? Who was an uncle or an aunt that looked with delight upon us, and how did grandma seem to fit us in with all the rest of the children she loved? Did grandpa even see us?

SELF-OBSERVATION: LIMITATIONS AND APTITUDES, SELF-ESTEEM AND FAILURES

Some of the limitations and aptitudes of our own personality showed themselves to some degree in our early days. We may not have recognized them on our own, and maybe not at all until our more reflective teen years. I, for example, was always more interested in mystery, virtue, and religious practice than anybody around me. I could work harder than most too, was ardent, serious, inward, frugal, and ambitious. I could memorize easily, yet find very few words for conversation with anyone at all. Where did these traits come from, and why did they descend upon me? Was there a power beyond us all that meted out such things? Was it random biochemistry?

The mixture of our treasured personal characteristics that we can only enhance to a degree, and our limitations we can only augment to a point, emerged in us through interaction with various people who mirrored them to us and showed us how they were pleased with them, or not. This part of our heritage, the self-esteem with which we face the world, meanders through our lives high and low, up and down, until the end. We eventually treasure ourselves, and then we don't again. Stories of what has tipped that self-assessment up into the proud or down into the swamps, reveal our humanness. When witnessed by kind eyes, a slice of healing for better caregiving relationships results.

RELIGION

The mass of religious practice, artifacts, buildings, teachings, leaders, and strongly held dogmas affects us all, regardless of whether we ever set foot in a church or were taught to pray. What have previous thinkers done with the primary questions human beings have asked for centuries about reality and our own purpose, meaning, and best directions for a fulfilling life? A piece of our spiritual heritage lies in

121

who tried to teach us about traditional religious culture, and how did we feel about them at the time? If there was church in our family life, who seemed to like it and who didn't? What did dad say about that sermon or that church we pass on the way to school every day? How did the Sunday school teaching on Jesus or Yahweh or Allah fit with what aunt Tillie said about it, and the tone of voice she used to convey her comments? What ricocheted off us on a philosophical level and what came into our depths about that part of human culture? What did we do with it? What happened when we tried to pray on our own? How did it feel? Did we try it again? And if there was no church in our initial background, what was it that other kids were saying about it? What did all that mean? What of substance did we take away from all of that early religious influence?

Pondering for meaning

While thinking does begin in childhood, it tends to focus on the uncontrollable more seriously later, beginning for most in pre-adolescence. We eventually ponder the Beyond and become more intentional about how we meet the uncontrollable as juxtaposed to how we learned about transcendence in childhood. When thinking for oneself emerges, gradually becoming full blown at some point in adolescence, it invariably has a major influence on a person's spirituality. Our own thinking generally bolsters the power of using logic to make decisions, and contributes leverage to academically pushy adults. It also offers us an entirely new way to relate to peers in serious discussion and for adolescent boys, even debate. Overall confidence can result. But it can also crowd out the *emotional* window on reality. Falling in love and the awe experienced at the sight of a daughter's face defy logic, as do many other human experiences that transcend thinking. Combining the two, thinking and feeling, remains a primary project of human maturity and can be remedially addressed in CPE.

REFLECTIVE QUESTIONING

Jose Willson was a sixth-grade classmate of mine in a religious school who began to ask sharp questions way earlier than the rest of us. He had always been smart. Suddenly he also became gutsy. Frail of body, mild of manner, clever and observant, he began to ask questions in classes that seemed obvious after he spoke. But none of the rest of us had made the connections he had made, noticing the incongruence between religious teachings and logic. His questions made some of us uncomfortable, but we also admired him as something of a hero, going gingerly against teachers where we could not yet go.

He had yet to discover however, that religion is not a philosophy, ruled by reason and hemmed in by logic. Religion at its best is about belief, practice, reverence or mystery, and the nurturing of the human spirit. While not bounded by human logic, it does however, for many of us, need to be reasonable or it is likely to be rejected as a viable factor in helping us cope with and enjoy the Beyond. Few if any of us have ever experienced religion at its best. In fact, most of us have experienced a mish-mash of inspiration and disappointment and deep wounding by the very organizations that are intended to help us spiritually. Religion is evolving, and on the way, it can exploit, discourage, disappoint, anger, and confuse.

The human development project of testing out childhood understandings with new-found ability to think for ourselves always produces mixed results. On the one hand, many of us simply cannot live our lives in blind faith. But on the other, most of reality defies logic. That is especially true of the richest aspects of human experience. Loving, for example, in any of its forms, is often mostly ignored by psychological researchers and theorists for its inability to be pinned down logically and researched carefully.

What are the stories of our beginning to cognitively evaluate our religious spiritual heritage? Where has the sporadic thinking taken us? What is the state of that process? How is it affecting our formation of a world view that includes visiting with suffering people every day?

DISCOURSE

Sharing our own ideas and opinions—in places that beckon forth discourse beyond the circumstantial and superficial exchanges of locker room banter, girlfriend chats, and cryptic Twitter sound bites—gets us beyond ourselves in the cognitive aspects of our spirituality. There we can pick and choose from others' serious thinking as we form our stances with and against various biases, convictions, and ideologies extant in society. Integrating our own views into that diverse world of opinions, facts, beliefs, biases, and prejudices seems necessary to developing an authentic identity of our own, a key component of a pragmatic spirituality. We learn an enormous amount not only about the world but about ourselves by discourse with others. CPE peer relationships provide a venue for that process to proceed on topics relevant to spiritual care.

SPIRITUAL STUDY

Focusing the mind on not only what we are thinking, but on how our opinions fit with what outstanding historical figures have thought about basic spiritual questions, currently and throughout the ages, constitutes the function of spiritual study. When directed by others—teachers, mentors, employers, for example—study of any slice of religious history expands perspective and broadens the base of knowing, building vigor into our spirituality. When directed by ourselves, however, such study takes on exponential power in doing so. The seeker finds much more than the compliant student.

Education in religious schools, theology courses, and theology school feed the need of some of us to explore the great thinking on spiritual issues that has transpired over the centuries in religious traditions. Like much of our heritage, that formation needs to be transcended by our measuring it against our experience of reality. CPE can catalyze that kind of thinking if it is shared and discussed in dyadic or group settings.

SCIENCE STUDY

Scientists exhibit less religiosity than some other professions, indicating that studying science affects the human spirit in important ways. Religion, however, is not the issue. Does studying science extensively bolster the human spirit with strength of conviction, perhaps enough to increase emotional resilience? Science as a method of inquiry excludes from careful consideration whatever cannot be measured. It uses imagination in the formation of theory, and commonly challenges early thinking about the world. Scientific study gives the impression of certainty to data, mathematics, and previously proven "laws" that can only be broken by indisputable new data. It is easy to get absorbed in that world of looking so closely at the material world that the reality of faces, affection, dreams, and emotional warmth fades for major periods of time. A scientific style identity can lend considerable solidity to one's ability to withstand very difficult crises. It may also shade the importance of intimacy, and human relationships in general, in human fulfillment.

MENTORING

Effective study eventually includes openness to mentoring. Specific teachers, professors, and practicing experts who are genuinely interested in you, as a person and as a developing professional, make a lasting impression on your practice and your spirit. They expand you, deepen you, and bolster your confidence and your poise. Like the savvy scout who leads your wagon train, they not only guide but also prepare you and contribute to the solidity of your professional identity. On the other hand, some mentors can be misleading and confusing ethically, and take you down valleys of styles of care that may not be as fulfilling as possible. Individual supervision and consultation with professional chaplains provide some of the best mentoring available for those exploring the possibility of a spiritual care career or augmenting a medical or nursing practice with spiritual care competency.

DISCERNING "EXPERTS"

Clearly religion, in its present evolutionary state, can be a mixed bag of support, inspiration, and invaluable guidance on the one hand, and manipulative exploitation on the other. Using your mind and your "gut" to discern which of the media pastors, witnesses, and evangelizers are more than charlatans or just good-hearted teachers may be a specific skill useful in caring for your own human spirit. Like the drug salesmen who frequent clinicians' offices, they typically bring good news and bad: helpful information about new and tested medications on the one hand, and self-serving propaganda on the other. Dealing with the ambivalence such salesmanship provokes inside you, even if it is good hearted, can jade your trust of spiritual leaders altogether. It is easier to avoid the entire reality of religion, or take refuge in cynicism, than to discern who actually is both capable of, and interested in, helping you spiritually.

Direct experiences of transcendence

Experiences of awe, both profoundly beautiful and shudderingly fearful, play a great, continuing role in shaping spirituality. Those events in which we become jolted even in adulthood, by what stops us, beats us, and nearly overwhelms us, make the uncontrollable vividly obvious. They impose themselves upon our ordinary way of being in the world, unpredictably at any time between childhood and oldest age. Events that shake us enkindle profound feelings, prompt us to do new and significant things physically, and make us think anew. By striking to our core, demanding we respond in some major way with all three of our basic human functions—mind, body, and soul— they invite us to further integrate them together in a different form of authenticity. In a very real way, they alter how we make decisions after that, and thereby shape our lives.

Each of these events is unique, but there do seem to be patterns to them as they erupt into most lives. This collection of experiences is so complex that studying them closely by vigorous research would produce data, but is not likely to ever give differential direction of care in evidence-based practice. Recalling and sharing only a few of them with colleagues, however, as in CPE programs, is likely to catalyze human connections for new understanding, resulting in unforgettable professional intimacy. Tears and laughter converse side by side when chaplain students do this in CPE.

GRIEVING

Nothing makes the uncontrollable more obvious than major loss. When somebody or something that you deeply treasured is pulled out of your life, the tragedy hits in a flurry of emotions and jumbled thoughts that make life different after that. The fact that you could not stop the loss makes the uncontrollable deepen in your conceptual world. Even if you fully or partially caused the loss yourself, the fragility of life is blasted into your face in an unforgettable way. One never fully "gets over it." It simply changes you. If you let it affect you in its own uniquely challenging way, it brings a kind of wisdom that appreciates life far more broadly and accurately than ever before.

Major loss is inevitable, a part of every life story, usually several times. Knowing that fact can be useful to assuage the feelings that loss evokes in a massive intellectualization. Allowing those feelings to beset you, time after time, however, makes life richer. Becoming morose, resentful, cynical, or jaded squeezes some of the best of maturing life out of you.

Some of the best grief is found in reminiscing with others who at least partially understand the specialness between you and the lost one. With or without tears, sharing the memories—sad, warm, angry, regretful, and funny alike—brings a kind of closure that celebrates but never diminishes. At some unpredictable point, after grieving enough, one finds gratefulness for the gift they were, the hurts they caused, the stretching of your life they precipitated, and the magnitude of the fact that they lived. If done well, grieving enriches our spirit and teaches us to grieve better next time.

If grieving your own losses is a particular spiritual skill, then helping others grieve is another one. A cluster of gentle, courageous questions and interpersonal responses, offered with sensitive timing and interspersed with moments of a lingering presence, beckons a person into a grieving state or facilitates that state for a kind of sharing that is uniquely healing and integrative. The outpouring seldom lasts more than 20 minutes.

RAISING CHILDREN

Still the high points of many lives are the births of each of one's children. That is however, only one spiritually enriching moment among thousands brought to parents by the people one helps into the world. There are innumerable events in parenting that can take you to the clouds or cast you into a dusty canyon. Once you have conceived them, there is never a day when you don't think of them many times, even after they leave your house. Other than romance and intimate loving, there is no more powerful contributor to the verve or one's spirituality than parenting.

Much of that benefit comes from experiences of confronting the limits of the influence you can have on these creatures dreadfully dear to you.

Sharing stories about children lights up a parent even when it only happens for a few minutes with a stranger in an elevator. About a quarter of all conceived fetuses end in miscarriage or other death before, during, or shortly after birth. Those stories are some of the most difficult for a parent to tell in any detail. They are also some of the most difficult cases for a chaplain to care for.

WONDER

The sharing of wonder between parent and child, even a toddler, no doubt launches a spiritual theme of celebration of beauty in the child all through their life. The intimacy of shared wonder turns off analysis, turns up delight, and allows the magnificence of the material world to wash over our being like a warm shower.

That is not to say we cannot be moved by experiences of magnificence all by ourselves. On the contrary, walking alone in a blizzard, taking in the ocean in any of its moods, or paddling a canoe alone against a brisk breeze, bring an intimacy with the natural world that is different from doing those things together with somebody else. But sharing beauty unites people, at the symphony, the theater, fishing together, or observing a total eclipse of the sun on Mt. Shasta. It bolsters the soul against the dreary and the tragic when they too arrive in their own time.

SCOLDING

In sharing on live TV the reason he was first attracted to his wife of 24 years, Canadian actor and humorist Michael J. Fox said that she was a colleague actress who boldly chastised him about an aspect of his irresponsibility that nobody else would do when he was flying high with success. The word scolding remains unpopular because nobody likes to be embarrassed for individual faults and failings. Scolding can be belittling, deprecating, and demeaning. But it can also teach in an unforgettable way and at the precisely best moment. Using an event to frame the importance of a particular action or circumstance, scolding can be a most loving action.

Barney was a perpetually grinning, 29-year-old, developmentally delayed environmental services employee of a small hospital, charged with cleaning the physician's locker room as part of his job description. He had become known as congenial and humorously extroverted. Six physicians were present one day in that locker room when Barney went on a tirade. Fixated by his furor, and secretly intimidated by his scold, they listened intently and laughed later. He was castigating them for their messiness, their irresponsible expectations of somebody to clean up after them, and likening them to impudent schoolboys. That story still lives among the leadership and medical staff of that facility.

We sometimes need to be alerted to dread by experiencing our parenting-ones and teachers as fiercely upset. The contorted faces and searing word flow cannot be mistaken as signaling that something here is of great importance. A toddler meandering onto a highway or near a precipice evokes such a scold that pierces the child more than cars whizzing at arm's length. When a patient rages at staff in a way that mentions personal details about them, the reactions of some staff members will be multiplied by vague memories of scolding endured in their childhood.

STARK REALIZATIONS OF MORTALITY

Watching a war movie with my older sisters at the age of nine scared me. When I acknowledged that to my siblings, they mildly but clearly berated my cowardice. That was the first time I remember being afraid to die. A year or so later, I remember being with two friends when we were invited by an older woman to come inside her apartment to see a dying man. Curious, we went. Flies, summer heat, and his labored breathing ignited my first real pondering of what it is like to die. Several other stories in which I was thrust into the feeling world of death and dying still rest uneasily in my memory.

There is a theme in every life, made up of events in which our own death came to the fore of consciousness. Those events stir us to look at the meaning of our own lives. Whether that reflectiveness ends after brief inner glances, shapes the seriousness of our life direction, or smolders for years in ruminative stewing, it tends to have some effect on the sturdiness of our spirit. It is worth a few minutes of sharing the specifics of that theme with colleagues. Shared reflections on how you want to die, in as much specific detail as possible, can also bolster a caregiver's spirit for calm interactions with seriously compromised patients.

INJURY, ILLNESS, AND HEALING

What a miracle, accepted without question, is the healing of skinned knees, finger cuts, and arm bruises in childhood. Watching a few days of the process from a burning elbow scrape, to scab formation, to flaking off on the way to complete healing, mystifies and gladdens the wounded boy. It works! Something is good about the world in which an accident, a stupid decision, an inflicted blow, and a mysteriously acquired flu, get better all by themselves. It takes considerable bad fortune, in the form perhaps of infections, complications, or serious, life-threatening illness later on, to overcome the positive bias these childhood observations of healing erect in our human spirits.

Those times do not, however, erase the fears of physical pain and horrible outcomes that swirl around hospitalized peoples' minds, invisible to staff members. Stories of our own serious hospitalizations and the events that precipitated them can come easy in an educational context of hospital care.

ROMANCE AND SEXUALITY

Sexual attraction and falling in love are not only spiritual in nature, but they constitute a major component of the spirituality of most people on the planet.[10] Romance is so soul shaking—both positively powerful and profoundly hurtful—that it brings both awe and dread directly into our faces and throughout our bodies. Tears generally signal soul contact, and tears of both joy and pain invade the romantic arena. Sharing the stories of your love life in a small communal context airs out some of our most private experiences, in humor, identification, and sometimes anger at hurts that seem so unnecessary. Yet much of our love life remains only within, not being intended for groups. When bits of a peer's love life are disclosed in CPE groups they are almost invariably significant.

ADMIRATION AND DISDAIN

Heroes and villains can inspire and discourage us during childhood and adolescence. Roy Rogers, Jerry West, and Jesus were the best of my early heroes. Modeling basic human goodness, the value of exceptional skills, and dedication to the betterment of humanity as a

---

10   Hilsman, G. (2007) *Intimate Spirituality: The Catholic Way of Love and Sex*. Lanham, MD: Rowman and Littlefield.

whole, they fed the making of a foundation for a positive, enjoyable, and fulfilling life.

People we come to either admire or disdain in adulthood can do the same thing. Once the time for heroes is past, people we see as exceptionally fine lend inspiration to a spirituality that is busy nurturing itself to overcome the necessary difficulties of living. Successful and principled colleagues, substantive celebrities, and mythical characters, like the priest and Jean Valjean in *Les Miserables*, still encourage the spirit of anyone who allows such people to affect them. They inspire and even motivate us with additions to our human spirit as it continues to develop through a lifetime.

ABJECT FAILURE

The failures in business and running for political office that preceded Abraham Lincoln's election as president of the United States would discourage almost any man. But as seen in many success stories—in athletics, publishing, business, and politics—failure can sometimes prod to greatness. Success probably always results from a combination of effort and good fortune. Neither suffices by itself. Failure can bruise, discourage, and misguide us into self-doubt. Abject failure is at least a minor theme to all lives, and a spoke in our spiritual wheel. When we can tell the stories of our nastiest failures, we have defeated their power to sway our sentiments when hearing the worst stories of the hospitalized people we encounter as caregivers.

Integration in ACPE programs

The goal of telling our stories in CPE can be seen as moving us towards integration. Graphic depictions of what ACPE programs are designed to do for participants can be centered around the concept of integration, making one out of many. Figure 4.2 illustrates how social and communal functioning brings personal resources to relationships effectively. We all carry fragments of religious and spiritual experience and their results in isolated solid beliefs, vague grasps of values, and partially held understandings from the mass of teachings and practices of the world's religions and spiritual traditions. Figures 4.2, 4.3, and 4.4 illustrate the process of integration in ACPE programs.

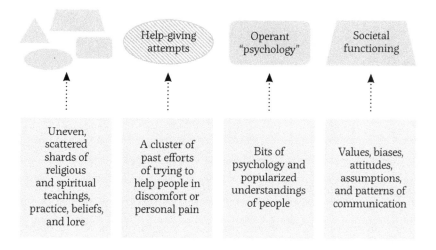

Figure 4.2 The integrative process of ACPE programs

Life-changing events like grieving major losses, falling in love, and facing our own death are examples of events and situations in which all of our major personal resources are pulled together to salvage what we can of our human spirit and embark on a new and mostly hidden path ahead. They compel us to use and revise what we ordinarily think, feel, say, and do, to cope with less serious happenings in order to meet this radically shaking one. CPE parallels those serious life eventualities in that it facilitates our use of our minds, hearts, and actions to process verbatim reports, engage one another in a level of professional intimacy in IPR groups, and speak clearly in individual supervision and group evaluation experiences.

As group members tell their stories of person history and patient care, they literally integrate themselves a bit more towards excellence as people and as caregivers. The circles in the graphics in Figure 4.3 move slowly together.

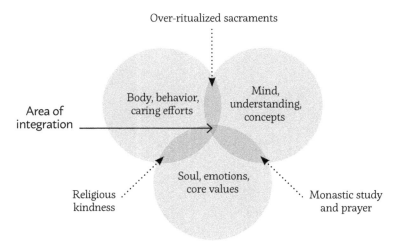

Figure 4.3 The integrative process of ACPE programs

All elements of ACPE curriculum and programming are intended to foster personal and professional integration in this way. Didactic and theological reflection sessions differ from lecture in that they are presented by practitioners who have integrated their theoretical understanding with their practice. Such sessions, over time, emphasize conceptualizing and cognitive reflection, lending to improved use of the mind combined with the heart to better understand and care for patients. Verbatim sessions challenge presenters and participants alike to use their thinking, feelings, intuition, and communication skills to comprehend a spiritual care relationship and engage one another in giving feedback and suggestions as to how to improve it. Open agenda sessions bring group members' observations, conceptual grasps, and in-the-moment efforts to care and confront in order to progress in skills of caring for people, their peers, and themselves. All of these involve some telling of historical and recent stories to fit them into the fabric of their human functioning and spiritual care relationships.

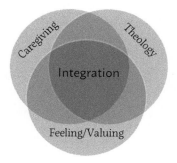

Figure 4.4 The partially achievable integration goal of ACPE programs

The hoped-for result is illustrated in Figure 4.4, in which, after CPE, there is a greater degree of congruence among these components of human personality. This is often apparent in CPE graduates in their level of communication authenticity, directness in relating, and even visual self-presentation that is seen by those who know them.

. . .

When a person is ready to make the leap into applying for an ACPE program, there are some considerations that will help them land one that roughly fits their personality, previous education, and place in life. That is the subject of Chapter 5.

5

The Limitations of CPE and Making an Application

The credit belongs to the man who is actually in the arena, whose face is marred by dust and sweat and blood; who strives valiantly; who errs, who comes short again and again, because there is no effort without error and shortcoming...

THEODORE ROOSEVELT[1]

While ACPE programs improve the interpersonal care of any serious participant, they have limitations. Some of these are *structural*. These programs are temporary. They are made up of at least 400 hours of combined education and patient care under supervision. An ACPE program is like a laboratory that exists for a specific purpose and is highly useful for defined measures of time. Laboratories are for experimentation and learning, and nobody

---

1   Excerpt from Roosevelt's speech "Citizenship in A Republic" delivered at the Sorbonne, in Paris, France on April 23, 1910. See the entire speech online at: www.theodore-roosevelt.com/trsorbonnespeech.html

lives in them. CPE programs similarly facilitate a concentration of focused communication for the purpose of helping people improve their care of other people in difficult times. One cannot extend the culture of CPE to a party, a family, or any other interpersonal venue in which there is no contract between the members to invest in a flow of interpersonal feedback for improvement of self-awareness and making changes in one's caregiving work.

ACPE programs are also set in *places of human struggle*. When they operate in other places, such as schools, factories, and public services agencies, where troubled people remain mostly submerged in work and social personas, the student caregivers are there for the times when problems erupt through that normalcy. There are struggling people everywhere of course, but CPE does not just teach spiritual healthiness. When it does so, it uses the context of human difficulties. The methods of CPE require the exploration of efforts to care for real people in real human trials. If everyone is in a happy place, eliciting the vulnerability it takes to ply real care becomes problematic. Such venues need chaplains, perhaps, but they are not the best places to recognize the radical changes that are needed for chaplain education. To challenge group members to consider the changes needed inside themselves to daily encounter the depths of human difficulty, settings where a major portion of the people are genuinely facing the worst human predicaments work best.

Some limitations of CPE result from the differences in *leadership* of the programs. The ACPE's certifying arm has long strived to confirm a basic level of integration, skill, and identity before authorizing its educators to practice in its programs. That scrutiny is vigorous but not perfect. Certified ACPE educators vary considerably in personality, clinical supervisory style, and convictions about how people best learn. Applicants can never be completely sure that a specific educator will fit their educational needs. They will need some initial trust to invest in the educational process and then a measure of adaptation to the uniqueness of the educators of the program to which they choose to apply.

The *group makeup* presents other limitations. ACPE educators intentionally try to select group members who are diverse, to maximize the spiritual perspectives for richness of feedback in the group. That is not always possible to the degree it is desirable. Programs are limited in their choices of students by the characteristics of those who apply. Sometimes the need to have enough students to conduct a group results in selecting a group member who is not personally ready for this style of learning. Some groups will be made up of fairly homogeneous members. A member of such a group will need to trust the process anyway. One can learn a great deal in any group of members who are well supervised and seriously pursuing the objectives and outcomes of APCE programs.

There are also *program* limitations. ACPE accreditation standards and processes are designed to require a basic level of quality of the methods and culture of a given program to adequately gel into the necessary educational milieu. Programs vary in the provision of these resources, depending on the patients served, the uniqueness of the staff who serve them, the financial sturdiness of the hosting facility, the mission of the facility, and the way in which these are combined and integrated into the CPE program. Such variations cannot usually be fully assessed by applicants before a program begins.

One of the most significant limitations of CPE programs can be the *attitude of leaders* about how much time it takes to make the internal changes necessary to ready group members for professional practice in their chosen field. The standard practice has been that for the vast majority of students it takes at least a year in addition to academic preparation to master the required competencies for certification as professional chaplains. Experimental programs and associations have proposed far less than that and are at risk of preparing people for a kind of chaplaincy that is limited to supportive care rather than the level of complex and specialized skills and practice competencies that interdisciplinary chaplaincy requires. As of the writing of this book there is no evidence-based practice of chaplaincy close to being widely verified by experience and research. Claims of such will need to be treated with caution by someone aspiring seriously to professional competence.

An applicant would also be wise to assess the *amount of distance learning* that a program uses in its curriculum. While technology has improved the availability of education and training over distances, a level of supervised practice face to face in the immediate presence of a clinical supervised group remains as essential to chaplaincy as it is to nursing and medicine. The combination of remote images and conversations with a peer group, processed writing, and dyadic interaction with an experienced clinical educator of a distance learning program can be highly successful. But they will be richer if also combined with considerable time for interaction in the immediate presence of one another, apprehending one another wholly, face to face, body language visible, group dynamics observable, engaging one another's spiritual care practice for direct feedback in the immediacy of being together in a room that minimizes distractions from outside it.

Curriculum can be a limitation. Research into the benefits of spiritual care for patients in healthcare settings has been growing and intensifying. More of this research needs to be focused on the quality of CPE programs themselves, their methods, their curriculum content as it actually unfolds, and their outcomes. Meanwhile, learning about published research can help a CPE group member acquire knowledge about the current state of the attempts to produce an evidence-based practice of spiritual care. But engaging CPE students seriously in their own research efforts can also seriously distract them from the hard and sometimes painful work of looking closely at themselves and their caregiving efforts that only sufficient clinical education accomplishes. The applicant would do well to assess the level of instruction included in the curriculum. How far does it lean towards academia in teaching about research, theology, psychology, or any particular faith group traditions? How early in a group member's CPE path does research or extensive reading get introduced? Immersion in clinical exploration of caregiving needs to remain the first priority.

Finally, there is the limitation of nobody being immune from the eventuality of *impairment.* As in any profession, certified educators can fall below the level of professional functioning adequate for practicing in the field of clinical spiritual care. The group member who suspects that this is happening to a staff member of the program is best advised to seek consultation with an appropriate official in the APCE to determine whether the complaint is best about the professional ethics, program quality, or practice competence of the troubling educator, and to seek assistance with considering whether and how to fashion an official complaint.

Admission to an ACPE program

Admission to an ACPE program is based primarily on submitted *writing* by the applicant about themselves, and an *admissions interview* by at least one faculty member of the program or a qualified substitute.

Some aspects of the applicant's writing that are likely to be considered as key by program faculty (certified educators in particular) are openness and a combination of succinct description and reasonably comprehensive disclosure. The reader of an applicant's material will likely be looking for words that lend the reader a feeling of knowing the applicant as a human being with awareness of how some relationships, and both successes and failures, have contributed to who they are. A minimum of this self-reflective ability can be expanded in the admissions interview and then later in the CPE group experience. Without it in adequate measure in application writing, however, that readiness for clinical spiritual education may be seen as lacking.

Selecting programs to which to apply involves several considerations. What is the program's reputation as far as you can ascertain? What is the supervisor's practice known to be like, as far as former students you know and other contacts can reveal? What issues of patients, patrons, or inmates are treated or cared for by the facility in which the program is situated? Is there diversity in the spiritual care staff there? Most decisions about programs are still made by geography, however. And that kind of trusting that an ACPE program will function with adequate quality will be a fairly safe component of a decision.

The *interview* may be face to face in immediate presence, or at a distance by technological connection. The time together with at least one faculty member is likely to emphasize emotional availability and conversancy about oneself as criteria for inclusion in the program. The interviewers will also be asking themselves, "How does this applicant deal with anxiety?" since learning in a care setting with people in any kind of treatment will be somewhat anxiety provoking for a student chaplain there. Questions like, "What has been this applicant's experience with failure, personal pain, and success at learning?" will be considered internally by interviewers. "What is the level of this applicant's empathy?" and the ability to expand it, will be too.

The applicant can also interview the interviewers to some degree. They can ask questions that they will seriously consider in their decision about accepting an admission invitation if it should come. As with a surgeon whom you are considering for a serious personal procedure, it is legitimate to ask such questions as, "How long have you been certified?"; "What would you say is your style of supervision?"; and a more human-to-human invitation like, "Do you like working here?"

6

Meet the Standards—Simplified

ACPE is the premier, DOE-recognized organization that provides the highest quality CPE programs for spiritual care professionals of any faith and in any setting. The depth of our training enables students to realize their full potential to strengthen the spiritual health of people in their care as well as themselves.

ACPE WEBSITE[1]

The ACPE objectives for programs and outcomes for students

As an organization the ACPE requires that curriculum for its Level I programs addresses the fundamentals of *pastoral formation*, *pastoral competence*, and *pastoral reflection*, without officially stating

---

1   www.acpe.edu

the meaning of those three terms. We can look at general definitions and etymology to address that lacuna.

- The term "formation" derives from the Latin *formatio*, meaning a "making or shaping." In the ACPE Standards it refers to bringing together diverse processes to make a person ready and able to be a practitioner, especially a professional practitioner, of spiritual care.

- The term "competence" combines the Latin *com* meaning together or against, with *peto*, to either attack or beseech. From the same roots comes the term "compete," suggesting that competence is what one needs in order to compete for something, a kind of preparation for excellence.

- The term "reflect" is the combination of Latin *re* meaning "again" and *flecto* meaning "to bend." It is a new reshaping of something already formed. In the ACPE Standards it refers to the professional's need to continually reshape themselves to stay competitive in spiritual care in an evolving world.

Putting these designations of outcomes together we can assume that the ACPE intent is: to continually develop curriculum towards an initial shaping of practitioners in a process that intentionally moves towards excellence, one aspect of which is deep motivation to continually reshape themselves for meeting the spiritual needs of people in a constantly changing pluralistic society.

The ACPE Standards distinguish *objectives of programs* from *outcomes of students*. Objectives are accreditation standards. Outcomes are certification standards. Accreditation is about programs while certification is about students. Outcomes can be used to discern and evaluate student progress in CPE. Objectives can be used to evaluate the programs as experienced by the students. The statements of objectives and outcomes use the same outline of pastoral formation, pastoral competence and pastoral reflection.

The word "pastoral," historically Christian, in a broad sense means "spiritual," and, in many contexts, has now been changed to that.

The ACPE Level I outcomes simplified

There are nine outcomes of Level I CPE, all aimed at the student gaining basic formational abilities for spiritual caregiving. They are formulated to delineate what the ACPE program student is expected to be able to do if they successfully complete Level I CPE, generally considered to be after finishing one, two, or three 400-hour units. Below are the standards (in italics) in their 2017 iteration, with interpretive explanations added. They are written as if the beginning of each statement is: "At the conclusion of CPE Level I, students are able to...".

PASTORAL FORMATION

The pastoral formation cluster includes three partially observable outcomes that focus on the student's gaining the kind of radical self-awareness that is invaluable in extensive patient care and the self-care it requires. These three outcomes are about the student's gaining familiarity with their own 1) religious/spiritual development; 2) human development; and 3) the ability to get the peer and supervisory feedback that produces them. Can they now:

> *311.1   articulate the central themes and core values of one's religious/ spiritual heritage and the theological understanding that informs one's ministry?*

CPE helps group members to become familiar with their own spiritual identity, beginning with being able to talk about what influenced their spirituality as it developed in childhood, matured in youth, and has been jolted and enhanced in adulthood. When asked, can they converse clearly about the people, events, practices, and beliefs that they have put together into their own unique array of ways in which they care for their own human spirit; that is, how can they cope with and enjoy the uncontrollable world? Can they own their "spiritual DNA" and tell about how they have reinforced, transformed, or rejected various aspects of it in their personal history so far?

> *311.2 identify and discuss major life events, relationships, social location cultural contexts and social realities that impact personal identity as expressed in pastoral functioning?*

This is essentially the same question as in 311.1 seen from a secular perspective. Can this ACPE program alumna talk openly about what life experiences have made them who they are today? Who were the people—parents, siblings, teachers, authorities, friends, lovers, offspring—who have most pivotally influenced the growth of their excellence as a person? What were the places, cultures, and events that have become sources of stories that accurately, if always incompletely, describe their life? Can they tell selected stories that demonstrate that development as they occur to them in conversations, or when asked?

> *311.3 initiate peer group and supervisory consultation and receive critique about one's ministry practice?*

ACPE programs aim to help group members learn how to get consultation that feeds back to them observations from peers and supervisors, about their personalities, their behavior, and their caregiving relationships. Getting solid and useful feedback can be more difficult than one expects. How well has this CPE group member done it? Can they talk openly about the best feedback they have received and how they educed it from colleagues and supervisors? Can they tell stories about their path of gaining skills for bypassing their own natural defensiveness to ask for consultation? Can they speak of times when they pondered critique and then worked towards behavioral changes to improve their care of people?

PASTORAL COMPETENCE

This cluster of four outcomes is focused on what the student is able to do with initiative, in the peer group and with patients, in order to optimize their learning in the program and contribute to the learning of their peers. Can they now:

311.4 risk offering appropriate and timely critique with peers and supervisors?

All members of a CPE group commit on some level to contribute to the culture of feedback, and that includes the most difficult aspect for most of them: providing critique of one another's care. It is easy for a peer to believe that their care of a given person was just fine, until their peers see or hear their depiction of it and ask good questions, verbalize their intuitive impressions, and offer suggestions. Can the peers now verbalize what they see in another person that they think would help them be a better person, or especially a better caregiver? Can they do it in a way that is likely to be heard and taken seriously by that person (critique) rather than merely criticize them (criticism)? The difference is crucial in this skill.

311.5 recognize relational dynamics within group contexts?

The time spent in interactional group education gives members the opportunity to observe group dynamics and the personal characteristics of their peers. This outcome focuses on how well they can now recognize such behaviors as the feelings, attitudes, communication patterns, values, and habitual assumptions of one another in the course of the group interaction. Watching one another closely and responding to some of what they see and hear, inevitably begins to instil this skill into their relationships with people. How well has that skill progressed?

311.6 demonstrate the integration of conceptual understandings presented in the curriculum into pastoral practice?

When professionals who are passionate about what they do present didactic topics, students benefit with some conceptualization or perspective that provides insight into patients and their peers alike. Can this student now be at least minimally articulate in answering the questions about that content session: "What did you learn from that and how has it been useful to you in your caregiving practice?" and "How would you critique it?"

311.7   initiate helping relationships within and across diverse populations?

The emphasis here is on two things: 1) developing rapport with many patients, and 2) respecting, and even treasuring, diversity among people. Group processing of patient conversations brings out the reality that all people in their essence are at least as good and valuable as the caregiver, and most are at least as smart. This outcome recognizes the various ways students learn to initiate, deepen, and bring to a close, helpful spiritual care relationships with most anyone. It also emphasizes the group member's attitudes and biases that may have remained hidden.

PASTORAL REFLECTION

The pastoral reflection cluster-of-two shows outcomes that describe what alumni students can now do differently in learning, one about the clinical method and one about setting and pursuing goals. Can this student now:

311.8   use the clinical methods of learning to achieve one's educational goals?

This outcome states how the student has grasped the clinical way of learning from supervised caregiving experience. What has been the student's attitude towards temporarily shifting their learning to a style that so heavily emphasizes experience over thinking, emotion over patterned behavior, and process over discussion? How have they related to their peers as colleague learners? What have colleagues said about their caregiving and their collegiality with them? How have they completed the requirements of the program? How have they related to the supervisor, the caregiving staff, and the other clinicians in the setting? In short, how well have they used the program for their own benefit and the experience of those maintaining professional relationships with them?

> 311.9   *formulate clear and specific goals for continuing pastoral formation with reference to one's strengths and weaknesses as identified through self-reflection, supervision, and feedback?*

Before arriving at CPE some students have become weary of setting academic and formation goals. But clinical education shows them that high sounding, culturally correct wording for goals may motivate little growth. After CPE they have learned how to set meaningful goals based on perceived weaknesses in their caregiving practice and their particular interests, and then how to work on achieving those goals. While some programs have softened the term "goals" to learning "themes," the results are quite similar. Has this student learned how to decide what they want to learn and then set out to learn it? What has their success been in doing so?

The outcomes of Level II ACPE programs

The Level II outcomes are used to evaluate the progress of Level II students during their involvement in Level II programs, and to some degree to assess students applying for admission for supervisory CPE programs. There is, however, no official occasion or process in which these outcomes are assessed as having been adequately completed. In a real sense they are seen as remaining targets for continuing education for the entire subsequent career of professional chaplains.

Movement from Level I to Level II CPE is the prerogative of the certified educator who last supervises them in Level I CPE. It is established through the certified educator's judgment documented in the final written evaluation (see Standard 308.8.2). Many programs require a group consultation with supervisors and experienced chaplains, for the student and the supervisor, before designating them as ready for Level II CPE.

The Level II outcomes use the same divisions as those in Level I: pastoral formation, pastoral competence, and pastoral reflection. They orient the student to more professional competencies after sufficient progress has been seen in their Level I CPE programs. They use the same beginning to the sentence: "At the conclusion of CPE Level II, students are able to".

PASTORAL FORMATION

312.1   articulate an understanding of the pastoral role that is congruent with one's personal and cultural values, basic assumptions and personhood.

This, the only formational Level II outcome, consists of what the group member writes and speaks on a philosophical level about an "understanding of the pastoral role."[2] To those of faith traditions other than Christian, that can be understood as being assessed by writing and speaking a theory of spiritual care, a statement of how one sees the helping relationship from a philosophical level considering the place of an ultimate power in it. It needs to be integrated with the writer's self-awareness of their own solidly held values, fundamental assumptions about humanity, and their own personality characteristics. It necessarily positions the role of the spiritual caregiver among other clinical disciplines with defined similarities and differences. To assess it as substantively completed, it would best be assessed in a multidisciplinary process.

PASTORAL COMPETENCE

312.2   provide pastoral ministry with diverse people, taking into consideration multiple elements of cultural and ethnic differences, social conditions, systems, justice and applied clinical ethics issues without imposing one's own perspectives.

---

2   This phrase may soon be changed organizationally to something like, "the spiritual care role."

This outcome addresses a conglomeration of considerations a spiritual caregiver needs to make in the course of their work that involves them keeping solid convictions about humanity while highly reverencing those of other people. It attempts to hang together very different caregiver functions, and in doing so highlights the complexity of the spiritual caregiver's role. It orients the caregiver to a level of mastery of medical ethics, ethnic differences, systems theory, the virtue of justice, and a high level of social awareness, requiring that these be considered in a professionally objective way. It is easy to see why there has not yet been a viable way to assess this outcome in a student. What can be notable is that one of these is glaringly missing. How much of a given area of egalitarian approach is necessary—for example of the boundless complexity of ethnic differences—has never been pinned down. Can it ever be? The fluidity of an applicant moving from one of these perspectives to another is a sign of adequately meeting this outcome.

> 312.3 *demonstrate a range of pastoral skills, including listening/ attending, empathic reflection, conflict resolution/transformation, confrontation, crisis management, and appropriate use of religious/ spiritual resources.*

This practical outcome asks to what degree this student has become skillful at various functions of caregiving that can be demonstrated in a clinically observable way. Can this student now listen well and widely, convey empathy, deal productively with conflict that involves them, be helpful to others in conflict situations, and use religious teachings and practices effectively? Can they confront solidly, objectively, and effectively? Can they convey empathy in most any caregiving situation? Can they listen intensively and extensively? Can they be personally helpful in the chaos of crisis situations? Have they put together this quiver of competencies in an integrative way that allows them to be counted on to function consistently as a spiritual caregiver in a wide variety of situations?

> *312.4 assess the strengths and needs of those served, grounded in theology and using an understanding of the behavioral sciences.*

Can this student use a practical level of familiarity with the behavioral sciences along with theological perspectives to assess people's spiritual needs?[3] Can they likewise appraise the strengths of a given person through conversation and reflection, for maintaining their own human spirit in difficult life situations? Can they evaluate a person's openness to referral with more than a single suggestion or question about motivation?

> *312.5 manage ministry and administrative function in terms of accountability, productivity, self-direction, and clear, accurate professional communication.*

This is a description of a professional, one whose consistent excellence qualifies her for the confirming process of association certification and being hired to do spiritual care work in regular collaboration with other professionals. Can this person be trusted enough to function productively with consistency in inter-professional communication, integrity of accountability, and without close supervision?

> *312.6 demonstrate competent use of self in ministry and administrative function which includes: emotional availability, cultural humility, appropriate self-disclosure, positive use of power and authority, a non-anxious and non-judgmental presence, and clear and responsible boundaries.*

CPE students are invited to see that what they have for patients is primarily their own personality. Whatever theological concepts they use to create a solid conviction about that, they can use it as

---

3   Hilsman, G.J. (2017) 'Spiritual Needs Common in Hospitalized People and their Goals of Care.' *Spiritual Care in Common Terms: How Chaplains Can Effectively Describe the Spiritual Needs of People in the Medical Record*. London: Jessica Kingsley Publishers, pp.97–151.

philosophical grounding as they consistently work to improve their relational selves to be better caregivers. This Level II outcome expands on that belief by outlining the various ways a caregiver uses themselves in caregiving. A level of emotional availability, for example, is needed for initial admission to most CPE programs, but a far greater ability to use one's present emotions in various ways, such as to touch people supportively, assure them verbally, confront them effectively, and otherwise function from one's feelings, is expected of one who is completing Level II CPE. Likewise, it is expected that that student has greatly broadened their cultural humility, becoming aware of their privilege and entitlement and at least some of their cultural biases. In addition, they monitor the level of their self-disclosure to fit the situation, not over-disclosing nor stonewalling when clear communication is needed. They manage their authority to neither be easily abused nor over-use their power to take advantage of other people in any way. They habitually carry an accepting presence that makes them highly approachable by anyone in caregiving contexts.

There is no widely accepted, reasonably objective way of assessing these functions, but some supervisors have identified indicators of progress on them that they use for writing final evaluations of Level II students.

PASTORAL REFLECTION

The three outcomes described here as indicating an adequate level of pastoral reflection have to do with the student's future functioning and growth as a spiritual caregiver.

> *312.7 establish collaboration and dialogue with peers, authorities and other professionals.*

Ease of interdisciplinary practice hallmarks the student who has mastered this outcome. Very few do this while still students and not many even accomplish it with excellence during their entire career. Seeing a student genuinely enjoying working effectively with other chaplains and IDT professionals is a sure sign that this outcome has been met.

> 312.8 *demonstrate awareness of the Common Qualifications and Competencies for Professional Chaplains. Note: The ACPE Standards and Code of Ethics supersede these standards.*

The *Common Qualifications and Competencies for Professional Chaplains* are a set of statements agreed upon in 2009 by representatives of the primary chaplain and educator certifying organizations of North America[4] to guide education and support of their members and aspirants. They have been augmented since then, and several of those associations have added standards that fit their specific organizations' ethos and values.[5] This outcome asserts that students who complete a Level II program are familiar enough with the chaplaincy standards and that they are conversant about what is in them when they are asked.

> 312.9 *demonstrate self-supervision through realistic self-evaluation of pastoral functioning.*

Self-supervision relies on a rather high degree of integration of rigorous self-awareness and self-observation that has been shown to be consistently accurate through peer validation and critique. It can be assessed by experienced peers who elicit from them extensive and specific descriptions of their caregiving, colleague, and personal relationships.

---

4   Originally these were the National Association of Catholic Chaplains, the Association of Professional Chaplains, The Association for Clinical Pastoral Education, the National Association of Jewish Chaplains (now NESHAMA), and the Canadian Association for Pastoral Education (CAPE), now the Canadian Association for Spiritual Care and Education.

5   NACC, NSHMA, and APC. To this date these primary chaplain-certifying bodies have not included in their collaborative association other similar entities who are seen to function with different basic values and standards.

The stated objectives[6] of ACPE programs

Clinical pastoral education was initiated primarily as a method of education, with little theory of why it worked. As it is in its present form it has evolved considerably from its early days. In a real sense, educational theory has grown up around it, and now supports it as conceived by supervisory students presenting their theory as a grounding for their supervisory practice. Pushed by society (The United States Department of Education which accredits the ACPE), its leaders have designed a set of objectives that its programs are required to pursue by ACPE accreditation standards. These objectives were used to fashion the ACPE Level I and II outcomes discussed above. They provide beginning ACPE interns, residents, and certified educator students with directions for understanding just what these programs are aiming to provide to help students learn spiritual care clinically. The essential wisdom in these program objectives is outlined below. You can find their current version online at the ACPE website.[7] *The interpretations inserted between them are the opinions and experienced questions of the author and not part of the ACPE standards and other official organizational regulations.*

PASTORAL FORMATION

> *309.1 to develop students' awareness of themselves as ministers and of the ways their ministry affects persons.*

This outcome is largely about fostering the growth of group members' spiritual care professional identity, their circumspection, and their ability to tune into awareness of how they are affecting the people around them. How is this program configured to promote the kind of feedback to students that improves their awareness of the aspects of their personalities and relational functioning that tend to seriously

---

6   Cf. ACPE Standards 309–310.

7   See www.manula.com/manuals/acpe/acpe-manuals/2016/en/topic/standards-309-319-objectives-and-outcomes-of-acpe-accredited-programs?q=Objectives. Accessed on 18/12/2017.

affect people, either positively or negatively? The proverbial "bull in a china shop" dramatizes how lack of awareness of one's own strength and blindness combine to damage individuals and valued structures. How does this program assist its participants to become alert to their surroundings and their inner workings enough for them to help and not hurt vulnerable people in their professional roles? What are the program's structures and values that are aimed at producing sensitive, profoundly reflective caregivers? How do the faculty and staff of this program demonstrate those values by their personal and professional behavior?

> *309.2 to develop students' awareness of how their attitudes, values, assumptions, strengths, and weaknesses affect their pastoral care.*

Attitudes, those solid personal stances we take towards almost anything, generally lie dormant within until they are made observable at unpredictable times, when the current conversation or event triggers them to surface. Then they may still remain unconscious to the one who holds them. How does this program help participants to become aware of their attitudes and unconscious biases that may skew their care of diverse people? How do the group members even come to understand how the terms "values, attitudes, assumptions, strengths and weaknesses" are understood by this program and how they affect the caregiving of participants? How do the staff of this program exemplify radical awareness of their own attitudes, values, and assumptions, identify their strengths and weaknesses, and manage their effect on the people around them? How have they processed those personality characteristics in their own lives and how do they monitor them with openness to feedback?

> *309.3 to develop students' ability to engage and apply the support, confrontation, and clarification of the peer group for the integration of personal attributes and pastoral functioning.*

Chaplains who function professionally need to be collegial rather than insular or merely congenial and gregarious. This objective suggests that ACPE programs help group members learn how to use groups to continue their growth as caregivers, especially when they may need to form those informal groups themselves when they are in practice as caregivers. CPE peer groups function as the central arena for learning, partially to help people learn how to use groups for their own development all during their careers. Groups need space that is free from interference and interruption for professionally intimate interaction in order to maximize group dynamics from which group me-mbers learn. How does this program provide such space and facilitate group members' use of it for their own learning? The purpose of these groups can be summarized in three terms: support, clarification, and confrontation. How do the faculty and staff members understand the importance of confrontation in clinical learning? How do they support group members emotionally when they need it and help them learn to support one another? How do they facilitate the processing for clarification and at least partial resolution of intra-group conflicts and conflicts that arise among staff members?

PASTORAL COMPETENCE

309.4   to develop students' awareness and understanding of how persons, social conditions, systems, and structures affect their lives and the lives of others and how to address effectively these issues through their ministry.

This standard says that ACPE programs help participants seriously ask the question of how the ways they grew up and were educated now affect their relationships with the people they seek to help. It assumes that all of us humans have "issues" related to our personal history and that these sometimes enhance our care and, more importantly, sometimes impede it. How does the program help a given group member get in touch with such realities as how their family's social status, ethnic heritage, and economic level affected their assumptions and attitudes about different segments of society, as they now may show up in their care of people in a diverse population of a pluralistic society? How do the staff and faculty of the program and the members of the department in which it functions, understand the importance of this factor and how aware are they of their own background? Can they talk about how they have developed this openness to diversity as something to be treasured rather than kept hidden for self-image management?

309.5   to develop students' skills in providing intensive and extensive pastoral care and counseling to persons.

One needs skills for caregiving, not just understanding. Does this program veer too far towards academic learning, or over-focus on skills for non-caregiving functions like fund raising, administration, or research? Where do the staff of this program stand relative to investment in the clinical ministry movement as a whole, rather than contributing energy only in the local program or regional/ national chaplaincy association organizational structure?

309.6   to develop students' ability to make effective use of their religious/ spiritual heritage, theological understanding, and knowledge of the behavioral sciences and applied clinical ethics in their pastoral care of persons and groups.

The spiritual caregiver needs to deal adequately with many sources of ambiguity in caring for people's human spirits. How does this program help prepare them to do so, especially regarding the various resources needed by very different patients? Is the spiritual grounding they have fashioned for themselves before and during the program well enough integrated into their practice that they use it smoothly with people of the same faith group as themselves? Can they use resources of other faith groups to some degree in a practice that lets people of that religion feel their care? Do they master enough behavioral science frameworks for some of them to be useful in understanding people and conveying care? Have they grasped enough group dynamics competence to contribute substantively and lead care-providing groups in organizations such as healthcare facilities and churches?

> 309.7   *to teach students the pastoral role in professional relationships and how to work effectively as a pastoral member of a multidisciplinary team.*

Spiritual caregivers need to work in collaboration with other professionals and be experienced there as genuinely contributing to the primary work of a professional caregiving team. Has this program involved its students broadly and deeply enough in interdisciplinary functioning so that they are able to begin professional collaboration with at least a minimally adequate level of the basic skills required? Do they have a positive attitude about other professions, understand their work accurately in general terms, and appreciate what they do for people? Have they substantially overcome authority problems that prevent them from growing to see themselves as true colleagues of other spiritual caregivers and helping disciplines? Are they still mostly critical of physicians and nurses?

> 309.8   *to develop students' capacity to use one's pastoral and prophetic perspectives in preaching, teaching, leadership, management, pastoral care, and pastoral counseling.*

This stated objective requires program managers to assist CPE group members to develop a voice in situations that threaten their pride with embarrassment if they fail. Spiritual care often needs some of what could be called prophetic action or risky advocacy. Continuing to learn in a clinical setting will bring group members occasional minor failures such as in team or colleague misunderstandings, over-reaching patient and interdisciplinary boundaries, ignorance of cultural norms, and hurt feelings from being ignored. These can be minimized to a certain degree in the CPE program, and highlighted as unavoidable so they can be sources of learning and not totally defeating when they happen. Does this program provide enough experience under supervision to accomplish that? Have the staff and faculty assisted that growth with their own advice, coaching, and example? Are students protected too much or too long from the realities of working in interdisciplinary settings so that they never grasp its rigor, pace, and stark communication culture as necessary, effective, and worthy of their learning adequate skills for collaboration? Has clinical care of people improved their preaching, enriched their teaching, and guided their management in a caregiving role? Do they grasp the difference between spiritual care and a counseling role, in the latter's characteristic time/place arrangements?

PASTORAL REFLECTION

309.9 to develop students' understanding and ability to apply the clinical method of learning.

Learning in this entirely new way challenges everyone who takes it on. In this program, is there enough orientation and initial support to make that transition progress effectively (though never painlessly)? Is the student left with too little guidance and accompanying supervision and to learn too much alone? Is there sufficient didactic material for students to integrate cognitive understanding with new experience? Students need resources and space to learn on their own, and supervisory assistance to learn in groups. How do they get to understand clinical learning and how to use it for their own development?

309.10 to develop students' abilities to use both individual and group supervision for personal and professional growth, including the capacity to evaluate one's ministry.

In CPE programs students learn alone, in dyads, and in groups. Is this program configured so that all three are combined adequately? Does this program offer or require adequate individual supervision, or leave students to function too much without that rich educational relationship that could assist their learning in the other two ways?

Is the small group actually small or large enough to become large group learning—more than six students per group—instead? Is there too much or too little reading, writing, and reflecting, allowed and facilitated, to help the student learn alone? How do CPE evaluation experiences help students to learn how to evaluate their own care of people?

For programs that offer education in specific specialty areas, there are three additional objectives. They are all written as if they end the sentence: "Where a pastoral care specialty is offered, the CPE center designs its CPE Level II curriculum to facilitate the students' achievement of the following additional objectives":

310.1   to afford students opportunities to become familiar with and apply relevant theories and methodologies to their ministry specialty.

Becoming a spiritual caregiver for a particular specialty unit or program deepens and broadens a student's clinical education experience. How well does this program provide resources for those students to incorporate theory and skills used in that specialty in order to expand on their caregiving abilities and be successful in it? In hospitals, obvious examples of specialty areas of care are oncology, hospice, mental health, palliative care, women's services, and renal dialysis. Prisons and addictions treatment facilities may be freestanding examples as well. Does this CPE program help students with specialized supervision, didactic instruction, and reading materials, as well as a certified educator with adequate experience working in that area?

310.2   to provide students opportunities to formulate and apply their philosophy and methodology for the ministry specialty.

Students providing care in specialty areas need to be able to actually minister to patients and families there, and conduct experiences for them that fit that specialty. Does this CPE program foster such experiences as spiritual care groups, and instructing patients and staff on spiritual care issues? Is there theory writing to be communally discussed or processed, possibly to include interdisciplinary staff members in the discussions?

310.3 to provide students opportunities to demonstrate pastoral competence in the practice of the specialty.

Does the program support "show and tell" events for specialty students to talk about their specialty work that includes participants from outside the group and CPE program?

The ACPE group member who becomes interested in certification as a professional chaplain will need to become familiar with the competencies required by the certifying body that best fits the student's theological or spiritual care philosophy and religious association membership. The competencies required of such organizations as the Association of Professional Chaplains, the National Association of Catholic Chaplains, and the Association of Jewish Chaplains, change periodically so need to be accessed on the internet for current versions.[8]

---

8   APC:www.professionalchaplains.org/; NACC: www.NACC.org; NESHMA: www.NAJC.org

Appendix

Sample verbatim format

St. Somebody Health System: CPE Program—Summer 2040
VERBATIM REPORT OF PASTORAL VISIT

Care Setting: Chaplain:

Number of Contacts: Date:

Length of Visit: Title :

I. **Introduction and Observations:**

Focus point: verbatim Interview: speaker (numbered)	Statement (as verbatim as possible)	Observations/ impressions (emphasizing emotions)
C-1= Chaplain		
P-1 = Patient		
C-2		
P-2		
C-3		
P-3		

2. **Summary:** Summarize the visit in a few sentences, emphasizing what seemed to happen in the patient and in the chaplain.

3. **Evaluation of Care and Recommendation:** What did you like about what you did and what would you like to do differently?

4. **Charting Note:** Type or copy the exact chart note you entered into the medical record.

5. **Spiritual Needs Identified:** What did this patient need and who would be best to provide it?

6. **Theological Reflection and Suggested Resource:** What sacred/poetic writings come to mind about this conversation? What are some other resources that could be used to understand this need and ways to address it?

7. **Cultural Implications:** What differences in culture—ethnic, social, language, sexuality, etc.—have serious implications for addressing this need?

Instructions

- Capture the verbatim conversation first.

- Type it and reflect on it in general regarding your efforts at caring for this person.

- Reflect on the other aspects indicated, and write your key reflections.

- Decide what you would like the group to focus on first as they help you explore it. Summarize it in the "Focus point" section.

- Write an introduction to the patient, including a brief description of them and their healthcare situation, how they appeared as you first met them, and why you first approached them.

- Complete your demographic information indicated at the beginning of the form.

- Finally, create a title that somehow intuitively fits this entire care event.

References

Adler, G., Jaffe A. and Hull, R. eds. (1973) *Letters of C.G. Jung Vol.1 1906–1950*. Princeton, NJ: Princeton University Press.

Agazarian, Y.M. (2004) *Systems-Centered Therapy for Groups*. London: Karnac Books.

Blackmur, R.P. (1983) *Studies in Henry James*. New York: New Directions Publishing Corporation.

Brown, B. (2015) *Daring Greatly: How the Courage to Be Vulnerable Transforms the Way We Live, Love, Parent, and Lead*. New York: Avery Penguin.

Brown, B. (2016) In Suresh Mohan Semwal. *Best Management Quotes*. New Delhi: Prabhat Prakashan, p.130.

Bruner, J.S. (1977) *The Process of Education* (2nd edn). Boston, MA: Harvard University Press.

Bruner, J. (2003) *Making Stories: Law, Literature and Life*. Boston, MA: Harvard University Press.

Cabot, R. (1926) *Adventures on the Borderland of Ethics*. New York: Harper and Brothers.

Clinebell, H.J. (1984) *Basic Types of Pastoral Care and Counseling: Resources for the Ministry of Healing and Growth*. Nashville: Abingdon Press.

Diamond, M. and Hopson, J. (1999) 'Learning Not by Chance: Enrichment in the Classroom.' In *Magic Trees of the Mind, How to Nurture Your Child's Intelligence, Creativity, and Healthy Emotions from Birth Through Adolescence.*. New York: Plume, p. 264.

Emerson, R.W. (1860) *The Conduct of Life,* Considerations by the Way. In B. Packer, J.E. Slater and D.E. Wilson (eds.) *The Collected Works of Ralph Waldo Emerson,* vol. Six. Cambridge, MA and London: The Belknap Press of Harvard University Press.

Fowler, J. (1995) *Stages of Faith: The Psychology of Human Development and the Quest for Meaning.* San Francisco, CA: Harper One.

Gillette, D. and Moore, R. (1991) *King, Warrior, Magician, Lover: Rediscovering the Archetypes of the Mature Masculine.* San Francisco, CA: Harper One.

Grossoehme, D.H. (2004) 'Patterns of unmet competencies by first time candidates for APC Board Certification.' *Chaplaincy Today* 202, Fall/Winter, 13–16.

Harris, T. (1969) *I'm OK, You're OK.* New York: Harper.

Helman, C.G. (1990) *Culture, Health, and Illness: An Introduction for Health Professionals.* Boca Raton, FL: CRC Press.

Hilsman, G.J. (2007) *Intimate Spirituality: The Catholic Way of Love and Sex.* Lanham, MD: Rowman and Littlefield.

Hilsman, G.J. (2017) *Spiritual Care in Common Terms: How Chaplains Can Effectively Describe the Spiritual Needs of Patients in Medical Records.* London: Jessica Kingsley Publishers.

Husserl, E. (1913/1967) *Ideas: General Introduction to Phenomenology.* New York: Collier Books.

Jung, C.G. (1973) Letter to Kendrig B. Cully, September 25. In G. Adler, A. Jaffe and R. Hull (eds.) *Letters of C.G. Jung Vol.1, 1906–1950.* Princeton, NJ: Princeton University Press.

Keys, R. (1993) *Nice Guys Finish Seventh: False Phrases, Spurious Sayings, and Familiar Misquotations.* New York: Harper Collins.

King, S. C. (2007) *Trust the Process: A History of Clinical Pastoral Education as Theological Education.* Lanham, MD: University Press of America.

Packer, B., Slater, J.E. and Wilson, D. (eds.) (2004) *The Collected Works of Ralph Waldo Emerson,* vol. six. Cambridge, MA and London: The Belknap Press.

Patton, J.H. (1995) *From Ministry to Theology.* Eugene, OR: WIPF and Stock Publishers.

Pruyser, P. (1976) The Minister as Diagnostician: Personal Problems in Pastoral Perspective. Louisville, KY: Westminster John Knox Press.

Rilke, R.M. (2011) *Letters to a Young Poet,* trans. Charlie Louth. New York: Penguin Books. First published posthumously in *Briefe an einen jungen Dichter,* Leipzig: Insel Verlag, 1929.

Roehlkepartain, E.C., Ebstyne King, E., Wagener, L.M. and Benson, P.L. (2006) *The Handbook of Spiritual Development in Childhood and Adolescence.* Los Angeles, CA: Sage Publications.

Rohrer, R. (2011) *Falling Upward: A Spirituality for the Two Halves of Life.* San Francisco, CA: Jossey Bass Publishers.

Schulz, C. (1950) Syndicated Cartoon. See D. King 'Charlie Brown Never Found His Little Red-Haired Girl, but We Did.' *Vanity Fair's* HWD Newsletter, November 6, 2015. Accessed on 11/11/2017 at www.vanityfair.com/hollywood/2015/11/peanuts-real-little-red-haired-girl

Thornton, E.E. (1970) *Professional Education for Ministry: A History of Clinical Pastoral Education.* Nashville, TN: Abingdon Press.

Further Reading

Hall, C. (1992) *Head and Heart: The Story of the Clinical Pastoral Education Movement.* Atlanta, GA: Journal of Pastoral Care Publications.

Hemenway, J. (1996) *Inside the Circle: A Historical and Practical Inquiry Concerning Process Groups in Clinical Pastoral Education.* Atlanta, GA: Journal of Pastoral Care Publications.

Patton, J.H. (1995) *From Ministry to Theology.* Eugene, OR: Wipf and Stock Publishers, p.96, first published by the *Journal of Pastoral Care* (1995). Patton is partially quoting here, Edward Farley (1975) *Ecclesial Man.* Philadelphia: Fortress Press, pp.71–72.

Subject Index

Author Index